LAND VALUES IN NEW YORK IN RELATION TO TRANSIT FACILITIES

BY

EDWIN H. SPENGLER, A. M.

Instructor in Economics

College of the City of New York

SUBMITTED IN PARTIAL FULFILMENT OF THE REQUIREMENTS

FOR THE DEGREE OF DOCTOR OF PHILOSOPHY

IN THE

FACULTY OF POLITICAL SCIENCE

COLUMBIA UNIVERSITY

NEW YORK

1930

LAND VALUES IN NEW YORK IN RELATION TO TRANSIT FACILITIES

BY

EDWIN H. SPENGLER, A. M.

Instructor in Economics
College of the City of New York

SUBMITTED IN PARTIAL FULFILMENT OF THE REQUIREMENTS
FOR THE DEGREE OF DOCTOR OF PHILOSOPHY
IN THE
FACULTY OF POLITICAL SCIENCE
COLUMBIA UNIVERSITY

NEW YORK
1930

Copyright, 1930
by
Columbia University Press

PRINTED IN THE UNITED STATES OF AMERICA

To

MY FATHER AND MOTHER

PREFACE

SINCE the beginning of the Twentieth Century, there has been a growing tendency to direct attention to the field of urban land economics. One of the pioneers in this work was Professor Richard T. Ely, who founded the Institute for Research in Land Economics and Public Utilities. Under his direction, important additions have been made to the literature on this subject.

Within recent years, the various monographs which have been published by the Regional Plan of New York and Its Environs have contributed materially to the available stock of information on the problems of city land values and city planning. These writings served to create in the mind of the present author, a lively interest in the changes which have occurred in land values in New York City. Suggestions offered by Professor Robert Murray Haig of Columbia University concerning the desirability of studying these land value changes, especially in relation to transit facilities, led the writer to make researches on this subject, the results of which are set forth in this present work.

The writer wishes to express deep appreciation for suggestions and criticisms made by all those who have had an interest in the preparation of this study. He is especially indebted to Professor Edwin R. A. Seligman of Columbia University who has rendered invaluable aid in recommending sources of information, in reading the manuscript and in making criticisms and suggestions for improvement. Grateful acknowledgment is also made to Professor Robert Murray Haig, whose excellent ideas have been responsible for the inception of this work, and whose patient examinations and comments upon the results of the investigations, especially in the early stages of preparation, have been most helpful. The advice of Professor Chaddock of Columbia University on the presentation of the statistical data is greatly appreciated. The services of Mr. Ralph Souter, who read the entire manuscript in its final form, and of Dr. Carl Shoup, who read the proof, are also acknowledged.

The author is indebted to a number of his colleagues in the College of the City of New York—especially to Dr. William H. Steiner, for important advice concerning stages of growth in Manhattan real estate, and to Mr. Harold Stein, for checking on the accuracy of certain statements in the chapter on The Bronx. Mr. Charles Hession should be given considerable credit for his untiring assistance in the work of statistical compilation.

The nature of this study has been of such character as to necessitate the aid of people outside of the academic circles. Advice secured through personal interviews and correspondence with men who are expert in certain subjects covered by this study, proved to be of great value. In particular, those who have cooperated in this respect and whom the writer wishes to thank are: Mr. Cannon, Dept. of Taxes and Assessments, N. Y. City; Mr. Philip H. Cornick, Natl. Inst. of Public Admin. Bureau of Municipal Research; Mr. Cullen, Dept. of Taxes & Assessments, N. Y. City; Mr. Cunningham, Dept. of Taxes & Assessments, N. Y. City; Mr. Hewson, Hewson, Carter, and Cottrell; Mr. J. Judge, Dept. of Taxes & Assessments, N. Y. City; Mr. Edward M. Law, Dept. of Law & Real Estate—Board of Transportation; Mr. A. Massett, Dept. of Taxes & Assessments, N. Y. City; Mr. Mungeer, Dept. of Taxes & Assessments, N. Y. City; Mr. C. E. Rightor, Detroit Bureau of Governmental Research.

The helpful services of the librarians in the Municipal Reference Library, as well as the kind cooperation of the officials in the tax offices of the City in providing access to the desired data, are also appreciated.

Part of the material herein contained was presented in the form of a report at a round-table conference on Land Economics at the forty-first annual meeting of the American Economic Association held at Chicago, Illinois, December, 1928. A greatly condensed summary of this report was published in the *Supplement,* March, 1929, Vol. XIX, No. 1, of the *American Economic Review,* pp. 49-53.

EDWIN H. SPENGLER

COLLEGE OF THE CITY OF NEW YORK,
MAY, 1930.

CONTENTS

CHAPTER I

PAGE

Introduction

A. The financial problem 13
B. Plans for special assessments 13
C. New York's present system of financing subway construction . 17
D. Underlying assumptions 17

CHAPTER II

New York's Modern Transit Facilities

A. A brief history of transit construction 19
B. A brief description of existing routes 21

CHAPTER III

An Approach to a Study of Land Values in Manhattan

A. A defense of the use of assessed valuations 25
B. Examination of value changes in the entire borough, 1905–1927 27

CHAPTER IV

The Downtown Business Area

A. The Wall Street District 30
B. North, to 14th Street 36
C. From 14th to 25th Street 46
In each of these sections, an analysis is made of land value changes, especially in the vicinity of transit lines.

CHAPTER V

The Midtown District (25th to 59th Streets)

A. From 25th to 40th Streets 51
B. From 40th to 59th Streets 56
C. East and West Sides 62

CHAPTER VI

The Central Park Area (59th to 96th Streets)

A. East of Central Park 66
B. West of Central Park 68

PAGE

CHAPTER VII

NORTH OF 96TH STREET 71

CHAPTER VIII

BOROUGH OF THE BRONX 79

CHAPTER IX

BOROUGH OF BROOKLYN 94

CHAPTER X

BOROUGH OF QUEENS 109

CHAPTER XI

CONCLUSIONS 126

APPENDICES:

A. A possible alternative to special assessments 135

B. CHARTS:

(1) Percentage Change in Land Value for Blocks Along the Broadway Subway, 1905–1929 139

(2) Percentage Change in Land Value Along the Lexington Avenue Subway, 1905–1029 140

(3) Land Values Compared with Bond Prices and with Land Values Corrected for Changes in Dollar Value, 1905–1929. 141

C. TABLES:

(1) Assessed Values of Taxable Land for all Boroughs, 1905–1929 142

(2) Percentage Change in Land Values of New York City, 1905–1929 143

(3) Increase in Value of Land in New York City, 1905–1929. . 143

(4) Final Complete Corrected Assessed Valuation of Land by Blocks for Manhattan. 145

(5) Summary. Values of Selected Blocks lying within Specified Districts in Manhattan 163

(6) Assessed Valuations of Land in the Bronx showing variations in Value Growth in] Different Areas for Selected Years 165

(7) Assessed Valuations of Land in Brooklyn for Selected Areas 166

(8) Assessed Valuations of Land in the Five Wards of Queens 167

BIBLIOGRAPHY 168

INDEX 173

CHAPTER I

Introduction

The costly construction of modern transit facilities has in recent years presented serious financial problems to municipalities which desire to build subway or railway extensions. In their efforts to raise the funds necessary to pay for such improvements, they have in several cases formulated plans for the levy of special assessments upon land in the vicinity of the new transportation lines. These proposals were brought forward on the grounds that accessibility is one of the factors which are responsible for property values, and that the affording of new transit lines to certain areas should reflect itself in increased values. The principle underlying the levy of special assessments is that the public improvement in question creates a distinct benefit or advantage to the adjacent property—resulting in a rise in value; that this increased value is then to be partly surrendered by the owner to help pay for the building of the improvement.

Upon this assumption a plan was developed as far back as 1911 in San Francisco, for the levy of special assessments for transit improvements. Since that time, three tunnels used in connection with street-car lines in the city have been financed by this method. In Colorado, in 1917, a tunnel was authorized for railway purposes, the cost of which was defrayed by money raised from the sale of bonds. Any deficiency which arises in interest and principal payments on these bonds may be met by special assessments upon the property values as of 1921. In the cities of St. Louis, Los Angeles, and Boston, recommendations have been made for subway construction financing by special assessments. So rapidly has this movement progressed in these cities, that there is little doubt that every effort will be made to secure the successful adoption of these plans. In Chicago, a committee of property owners who would be affected by a subway plan such as was contemplated recommended a special assessment levy to cover the cost of construction. In Detroit a comprehensive plan was proposed involving street-car systems which would be submerged along parts of their routes, as well as a combination elevated and subway line. The estimated cost was figured at ninety-one million dollars. The financial plan called for an issue of full-faith and credit bonds of the City of Detroit, and the balance in mortgage bonds. It also authorized a system of ad valorem taxation to pay for about 17 per cent of the cost. It was provided that the bond issues should be retired through the levy of special assessments on " property benefited—provided, however, the Common Council shall determine that sufficient benefit has accrued to private property as to render it reasonable to levy such assessments. . . .[1] The proposal was submitted to the voters for approval at the election on April 1, 1929, but was overwhelmingly defeated.

New York has not been without similar suggestions. In fact, New York was the scene of early activity favoring such methods. As early as 1908, a transit committee of the New York City Club made a study of the influence of the New York subway upon land values. Their discovery in this investigation was that territories which had had no previous transit facilities experienced increases in values above their normal growth, that were several times greater than the entire cost of construction of the subway extensions. The result of this study was that a series of changes were made

[1] *Detroit Free Press*, March 12, 1929. Reprint of a section of the ordinance, p. 13.

in the New York law—Chapter 888 in 1911, and Chapter 545 in 1915,—which gave the city of New York the right to construct rapid-transit lines by resort to special assessments.

Since that time, several unsuccessful attempts have been made to use this power in financing the construction of new subway lines in the City. One proposal was in connection with the Utica Avenue subway in Brooklyn; another, with reference to the removal of the Sixth Avenue elevated system, and the building of a subway; and a third, in connection with the new City Subway system, now under construction. In all three cases, especially the latter, considerable time and expense were devoted to studying the methods to be employed in levying these assessments. In the preliminary studies for the new City, or Independent Subway for Eighth Avenue, John H. Delaney, Chairman of the Board of Transportation ordered the preparation of a plan, together with tables and maps which would show the benefited areas around the new subway, and the methods for their assessment. These areas were blocked out, and the precise amount of the assessment levy on each parcel of land was calculated; as is usual in the practice of the levy of special assessments, the assessment areas were designed on the basis of the assumption that the degree of benefit varies inversely with the distance of the site from the improvement. At the meeting of the Board of Estimate, whose sanction was needed before the plan could go into effect, the proposal was voted down, and construction proceeded without the special assessment device.

The chief contention which has been raised in New York City in each of these cases has been that owners question why they should shoulder the entire burden of paying for a subway, when the general taxes toward which they already contribute, go to pay the principal and interest on bonds that have been floated to pay for other subways. This problem naturally does not arise in a newer area which has not yet built any transit lines.

The most recent study which has been made on this proposal, is the report of the North Jersey Transit Commission to the State of New Jersey—1927. The report of this commission gives considerable attention to the growth of property values adjacent to transit routes, and to the use of special assessments in financing the cost of construction of additional transit facilities in northern New Jersey.

All of these proposals rest upon the idea that subway construction will undoubtedly have the effect of increasing the value of property lying in the area through which it passes.

This point of view is clearly developed in a report by the Subway Advisory Commission of Chicago, in which the statement appears: [1] "That local benefit arises from urban transportation systems is so indisputable as not to warrant further argument or illustration. The degree may and does vary—the fact of local benefits does not." Quoting Mayor Dever of Chicago, the same thought is evidenced: [2]

> While subway construction is the most expensive type of railway construction, the building of subways in other cities has *invariably* proved highly profitable to persons owning adjoining property. . . . The fact that property adjacent to the subway is enormously benefited, and its value stabilized, is so well known that property owners along all the downtown streets in which subways might be built, will, in my opinion, be more than willing to cooperate with the City in hastening subway construction.

In Detroit, a report to the Mayor, in 1929 stated that a result of the transit facilities proposed in that city would be to give

> a direct benefit to all property served by the rapid transit system, and made more accessible to more persons because of the improved transportation service that is given. This benefit

[1] *Report of the Committee on Rapid Transit No. 106,* American Electric Railway Association, 1928, pp. 14-15.

[2] *Ibid.*, p. 15.

expressed in increased usefulness of property (through higher rents, increased business, etc.) and in increased value can be bought and sold. It is a direct marketable benefit.[1]

An extreme view on the effects of transit upon land values was recently stated in an article by Mr. R. L. Duffus, in which he said: "Subways and elevated lines themselves create values which are reflected in larger tax revenues. An elevated line, it has been found, will approximately double neighboring land prices while a subway will multiply them by from four to twelve times." [2] If this statement were accepted as it stands, without reservation, it would almost appear profitable for landowners to go into the business of wholesale transit construction.

In an article [3] by John H. Delaney, appears the statement:

> The investigation conducted by this Board (Board of Transportation) discloses that the existing rapid transit lines have at least doubled the value of property in all outlying areas served, and that property located at new stations has everywhere gained three times its earlier value. All property located upon or near a rapid transit line is increased in value by such a convenience. *All the city is benefited by every addition to its transit facilities.*

Acting in harmony with the view presented in this last sentence, the City of New York is now adopting the policy of deducting twenty-five millions of dollars a year from the real estate tax revenue, upon the hypothesis that all of the real estate (land and buildings included) will benefit by the addition of the new subway route, and will increase so

[1] Report of the Street Railway Commission and the Rapid Transit Commission to Hon. John C. Lodge, Mayor, February, 1929, Detroit, Mich.

[2] *The New York Times*, Sept. 22, 1929, "Our Great Subway Network Spreads Wider," R. L. Duffus, p. 4xx.

[3] "New York City's New Subway System," John H. Delaney, Chairman of the Board of Transportation, *Bulletin of the General Contractors Association*, December, 1923.

rapidly in value that this outlay can be paid entirely out of ordinary increased tax revenue due to the rise in value of the property.

In view of the fact that these various commissions and public bodies appear to be proceeding upon the assumption that extensions of systems of rapid transit are directly and inevitably responsible for urban land-value increases, it is of interest to examine some of the data on the course of land values with respect to increases in transit facilities in New York City.

CHAPTER II

New York's Modern Transit Facilities

The last two decades have witnessed a remarkable growth in subway construction within the New York area. This expansion has been in the four boroughs — Manhattan, Bronx, Brooklyn, and Queens.

At the time the City Club made its study in 1908, the subway system of New York ran from the Battery to Grand Central Station, then across 42nd Street, where one branch continued up to 242nd Street, and the other went to Bronx Park. The junction for this fork was placed at 96th Street. This service had been opened as far as 145th Street and Broadway in October 1904. Full service to Van Cortlandt Park was opened in August, 1908. The subway went to South Ferry in 1905, and after the tunnel was completed under the East River, was extended to Borough Hall, Brooklyn, in 1908.

Besides these lines, the Interborough operated all the elevated railroads in Manhattan. The first permanent elevated structure had been built on Ninth Avenue extending from the Battery to 21st Street. This began running in 1869, and was operated by cables drawn by stationary engines. By 1876, the Second, Third, Sixth, and Ninth Avenue roads were operating, and in the early years of the next decade service was extended into Harlem. In 1902, these roads which had first been operated by steam engines, were electrified.

Since 1908, numerous transit extensions have been made in Manhattan. In July, 1911, contracts were awarded for construction of the new Lexington Avenue subway and in the same month, work was begun at Lexington Avenue and 62nd Street. In 1913 contracts for a dual system of rapid transit were signed by the City, with the Interborough, and the New York Municipal Railway Corporation. This provided for

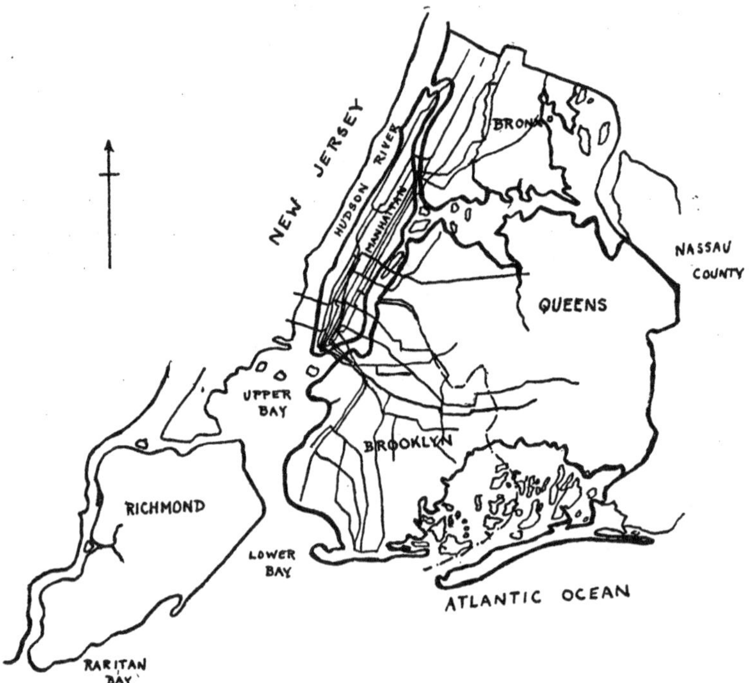

NEW YORK CITY

MAP SHOWING THE FIVE BOROUGHS AND INDICATING RAPID TRANSIT FACILITIES.

the operation of the new Seventh Avenue subway, the Lexington Avenue line, the old Park Avenue line, the Steinway Tunnel under 42nd Street, and for the Broadway subway from the end of the island to 59th and 60th Streets, and along those streets to the East River, and over to Queens.

Three important subway extensions resulted from these arrangements: A new route connecting Manhattan with Brooklyn and Queens ran under Broadway to 59th Street. The main line along Broadway as far as Times Square, was operating in 1918, but the extension to 59th Street on the north, and the connection to Brooklyn on the south, did not open until 1920 when the tunnels to Queensborough Plaza, and the Montague Street Tunnel to Brooklyn, were completed. A new subway was built along Seventh Avenue and connected with the old subway at 42nd Street. The old subway which ran along Park Avenue was extended from Grand Central Station northward, along Lexington Avenue, and into the Bronx. These two links, which made of the old subway what was known as the "H" system, were opened in 1918.

In 1924, the 14th Street Eastern line was opened from Sixth Avenue and 14th Street in Manhattan, to Bushwick Avenue in Brooklyn. In 1928, this line was able to establish through connections from Eastern Parkway in Brooklyn, to the Broadway (B.M.T.) Subway in Manhattan.

The Bronx had the Second Avenue elevated extension from Manhattan as a transit arm at the time that it received its first subway. This elevated line had been constructed in 1888 and helped to bring about an early development in relating the affairs of this borough with those of Manhattan. Of course, the New York Central lines had also contributed toward this effect. The first Bronx subway was opened in 1904. It extended along East 149th Street to Westchester Avenue and from there, it became an elevated line, as far as Bronx Park. In 1906, a tunnel under the Harlem River was opened, which connected this route with the Lenox Avenue branch of Manhattan's subway. (The western branch of the Manhattan line extended to Van Cortlandt Park). The famous Dual Contracts of 1913 which did so much for transit development in New York City, gave the Bronx a large increase in its transit lines. On the basis of this agreement, construction was started which resulted in the opening in 1917, of an extension of the first subway via an elevated line from Bronx Park along White Plains Road, as far north as 241st Street. In the same year, the Jerome Avenue branch of the Lexington Avenue subway of Manhattan was put into operation. This opened direct connection from Woodlawn to downtown Manhattan. Finally, in the following year, a new line, partly subway and partly elevated to Pelham Bay Park, along Southern Boulevard and Westchester Avenue, provided another link feeding into the Lexington Avenue subway system of Manhattan.

The opening of service to Borough Hall, in 1908, from the Lexington Avenue line in Manhattan gave Brooklyn its first subway. Furthermore, it marked the beginnings of the coordination of activities of the several boroughs of the Greater City, through transit links. In mileage of track, Brooklyn could, at the time, vie with Manhattan in view of its large network of elevated lines that had been built near the end of the preceding century. These included the old Sea Beach Line, the Fulton Street system, the Myrtle Avenue, Lexington Avenue and Broadway elevated roads, and the Fifth Avenue route, as well as the Long Island Railroad from Atlantic Avenue, Brooklyn, to Jamaica. This road was electrified in 1905.

Later in 1908, the subway was extended to its terminus at Atlantic Avenue. Since this connected it with the Long Island Railroad terminal, it enabled a fairly large area in Brooklyn to obtain rapid transit to Manhattan.

Prior to the dual system negotiations, construction work was begun on a Fourth Avenue subway route, the plan being to link this with Manhattan in the future. As an outcome of the Dual contracts of 1913, it was provided that the

Brooklyn company (B.M.T.) was to build a tunnel from Broad Street in Manhattan, to Montague Street in Brooklyn, and to connect the Fourth Avenue line under construction via the tunnel to its Broadway subway which would be erected in Manhattan. In 1915, this route was opened as far as 65th Street in Brooklyn. From here, the reconstructed Sea Beach line was opened to Coney Island the same year. In 1926, the Fourth Avenue line was extended to Fort Hamilton.

The new Culver line was placed in partial operation in 1916 and finally completed through to Coney Island in 1920. This is an elevated road, as is also the West-end line which was opened for service to Coney Island in 1917. The Brighton Beach road opened in 1920. This made the fourth system which was extended into this part of Brooklyn within five years. At its southern extremity it was connected with the other three routes.

The Interborough Company in the meantime had constructed a new tunnel under the East River for the purpose of connecting its new West-side subway in Manhattan, with its Brooklyn lines. This was opened in 1919. It provided service to Clark Street, Brooklyn and from there, to Borough Hall, and thence along the old line already existing. From the Atlantic Avenue terminus, extensions were made to Utica Avenue in 1920 and New Lots in 1922. A branch along Nostrand Avenue to Flatbush Avenue was opened in 1920.

As was already mentioned with reference to Manhattan, the 14th-Street Eastern line was finally opened for full service from Eastern Parkway, Brooklyn, to Manhattan in 1928.

Queens was not very fortunate with regard to securing rapid transit facilities. Aside from the Long Island Railroad system, which provided routes to Jamaica and Queens, and to Long Island City, and Whitestone, and the short extension of the Myrtle Avenue elevated line of Brooklyn, Queens did not get any rapid transit lines until the Dual Contracts were made. According to the plans in these contracts, Queens obtained two elevated lines—one extending north in Second Avenue, Long Island City to Ditmars Avenue, Astoria, and the other, along Queens Boulevard and Roosevelt Avenue to Corona. It was arranged that these lines should meet at Queensboro Bridge Plaza,—a junction station for both B.M.T. and I.R.T. lines. From this point, it was provided that the Interborough would proceed to Grand Central via the old Steinway Tunnels, and the New York Municipal Railroad would connect by tunnel to 59th Street in Manhattan. This subway was completed through to Queensboro Plaza in 1916 and operation to Astoria and Corona began in 1917. The B.M.T. connection with Manhattan, however, was not completed until 1920.

The Dual contracts also provided for an extension of the Fulton Street line to Lefferts Avenue in Richmond Hill; and for an extension of the Broadway line from Cypress Hills to Jamaica. The former came into service in 1915. The latter opened in 1917 and 1918.

An elevated line was opened from Corona to Flushing in 1928.

The new subway to run along Eighth Avenue and 53rd Street in Manhattan, and with long extensions connecting the four boroughs, is now under construction. A part of this will open in 1931.

The maps provided throughout the text, indicate the routes referred to in this brief summary of the development of New York's present rapid transit system. Surface transit lines and motor-bus facilities have not been specifically considered in this study.

CHAPTER III

An Approach to a Study of Land Values in New York City

As a basis for this investigation, assessed valuations compiled by the Department of Taxes and Assessments of New York City were used. While actual market values might be deemed to be a more ideal standard for a study of this kind, there are several reasons why the assessed valuations can be justified. First, there is the question of available data. Market values are available only for such parcels as have been sold recently, and even then it is very often difficult to obtain such information. Furthermore, in many of the recent sales for which reliable data exist, the information is somewhat unsatisfactory in that it refers to forced sales at auction. Again, there is much property which has not been sold for many decades. The assessed valuations are compiled for each parcel on an annual basis. Secondly, market values may be temporarily inflated through speculative selling; assessed valuations usually err on the side of conservatism. Thirdly, assessed valuations are forced to the upper limit through the need of the City for revenue; they are kept from going disproportionately high through the practice of permitting individual appeal by the property owners. Moreover, market values are usually stated for land and buildings combined, unless the parcel in question is a vacant lot, whereas the assessment figures separate the value of unimproved land from the value of land with improvements. In a study of this kind, of course, this mode of separation is especially convenient.

As a basis for the study of relative changes in land values, the assessed figures seem to be justified. The tax law requires that all real estate liable to taxation shall be assessed at its full and true value as the assessors would appraise the same in payment of a just debt due from a solvent debtor. The State Equalization Board of New York estimates the average assessed valuation figures to be within ninety-three per cent of the actual land value. In an assessment study made along the new Independent lines of the City, in 1925, Mr. A. M. Schermerhorn defended the use of assessed values for this purpose as follows: [1]

Assessed values are used because there are no other criteria extant, nearly as universal, systematic and conservative. Assessed values, while not keeping pace with every individual change in market value, are free, however, from extremes of valuation which result from elements very remote and speculative, and depend quite frequently on what might be called " booms " or sporadic market psychoses. They are legally supposed to represent fair market value, and for purposes of comparison, their use in any assessment study is peculiarly proper.

This point of view is also seen in one of the recent reports of the City Committee on Plan and Survey, as follows: [2] " The technique of real estate assessment and the organization of the Department of Taxes and Assessments in New York City have for many years been the occasion of just pride among the citizens of the City. In these respects New York City has set the standard for the entire country."

[1] *Report*, Aug. 31, 1925. Avery M. Schermerhorn, Assessment Study No. 1 made by direction of the Chairman of the Board of Transportation.

[2] *Finances and Financial Administration of New York City*, recommendations and report of the sub-committee on budget, finance and revenue of the City Committee on Plan and Survey, Rogers McBain & Haig, 1928, p. lxvii.

Nevertheless, a word of caution is necessary. Although assessed valuations may be used to indicate relative changes in land values for areas over a period of time, they cannot be relied upon at all times as indicative of absolute values for individual parcels. It is known that in many cases market values are frequently appreciably higher or lower than the assessed valuations. These individual variations, however, should not serve to disqualify the use of these figures for purposes of comparison of changes or for use in noting trends of advance or decline.

The year 1905 has been chosen as a starting point, inasmuch as it was in this year that the assessors of New York City for the first time, separated the land values from "land and improvements." This year is also significant as practically the date of beginning of subway history of New York, for the first subway was opened in the Fall of the preceding year.

For the twenty-four year period, 1905-1929, the land values in the City of New York increased by almost 160 per cent. This growth was not, however, spread uniformly over the period. From 1905 to 1911, there was a real-estate boom, and heavy buying activity. In this period, total land values increased by about 47 per cent. Then came an interval when land values were virtually marking time, making an increase of somewhat more than one per cent from 1911 to 1915. With the opening of the World War, rising prices of building materials were accompanied by less activity in real estate developments. Furthermore, funds were being diverted into channels other than real estate. Where rentals were fixed in leases running for a number of years, the incomes to owners became relatively smaller in view of the decline in the purchasing power of the dollar. This had an adverse effect upon land values, and an average decline of minute proportion was indicated for the entire City by the year 1919. The net effect of this period was that land values in 1919 were virtually the same as those of 1911. A recovery then followed, at first slow, but rapidly gaining momentum with heavy post-war demands, building shortage, rising rentals, falling interest, increasing funds for investment, and so on, so that in the ten years following 1919 a gain of over 75 per cent was recorded.

This general picture does not tell the whole story, however, for during this period land values in some parts of the City were steadily declining, in other parts, steadily rising, and in still others, rising and falling.

The variability in the changes produced in land values in different parts of the City during this period is clearly illustrated in Table 2 in the appendix. While the total city showed a gain of about 160 per cent for the quarter century, Manhattan shared in this increase to an amount of less than 100 per cent, while Queens witnessed a gain of more than 1000 per cent over its 1905 value. Furthermore, the drop of almost five per cent in Manhattan land values during the war was almost counterbalanced by gains in all of the other boroughs during this period. Table 3 presents another angle of approach to this problem. It will be seen by comparing Tables 2 and 3 that while Manhattan showed the smallest percentage of increase in land value from 1905-1929, almost half of the total value increase for the City was contributed by that borough; whereas Queens, which indicated the greatest rapidity in growth, supplied less than 16 per cent of this total gain. This is, of course, explained by the fact that the original value for Manhattan was much higher than that of the other boroughs and consequently a small percentage increase of this value represents a considerable contribution to the total for the City.

In order to examine more closely these changes in the value of land, each of the boroughs affected by New York's rapid transit system will be discussed separately. The greater part of the study will be devoted to a detailed consideration of Manhattan; for this borough, besides being the center of the City's transit system, presents a most varied array of the many types of sections to be found in a mature city. The other boroughs will be treated in more general fashion.

In order to facilitate the study of Manhattan, the island may be divided into two groups of territory—the central core, from Third Avenue to Ninth Avenue, in which lie the bulk of the transit lines constructed within the last quarter century, and the periphery on the East and West sides where no notable additions in transit lines have been made since 1900. An exception to this general division is the Broadway-7th Avenue line of the I.R.T. which follows Broadway north of 42nd Street, and proceeds steadily westward along Broadway, the most westerly avenue north of 106th Street. This line, constructed in 1905 is the only subway now serving this area. Most attention will be focused on the more central sections of the island, although the outside areas will be of interest, especially for comparative purposes.

An interesting assortment of changes in land values is depicted in this central core of the island in the years following 1905. To best illustrate the nature of these changes, this area in turn, has been divided into several sections. These may be designated conveniently as follows:

1. The Downtown Business Area
    a. The Wall Street District
    b. North, to 14th Street
    c. From 14th to 25th Street
2. The Midtown District (25th to 59th Streets)
3. The Central Park Area (59th to 96th Streets)
4. North of 96th Street

CHAPTER IV

The Downtown Business Area

THE extreme lower tip of Manhattan Island is what is usually referred to as the financial district. With Fulton Street as the northern boundary, this small segment of the island can, perhaps, be looked upon as a section, which has held its ground for a certain use longer than any other piece of land in the City. With the exception of the earliest Colonial days, when State Street, Pearl Street, and Bowling Green were the fashionable residential sites, this region has been devoted to finance and commerce. The steamship and consular offices were located at the Battery at a very early date, West Street was a market section in the Seventeenth Century, and Broad Street had its first stock exchange at the Stone Street crossing in 1670. The present Stock Exchange dates its origin to a formal organization formed in 1792 at 68 Wall Street. The opening of important commercial and financial offices in the neighborhood of the Exchange, soon made this the " business district " of Manhattan.

The first of the modern rapid transit conveniences which were constructed here were the elevated lines running from the Battery to the East and West sides of the island, along Pearl Street on the East, and along Trinity Place and Greenwich Street on the West. The first subway, opened in 1904, proceeded down Broadway to South Ferry. In 1905, therefore, this area was already served by four subway stations and eight elevated stations. Nine new subway stations on four new lines have since been added, and the new Eighth Avenue Subway under construction will place an additional station at Fulton Street, extending from Nassau to William Street. This makes a total for this little area, of twenty-two points of access to rapid transit lines.

For the period 1905-1929, land values in this section show an average gain of 60 per cent or approximately at the rate of two per cent per annum. This is somewhat below the

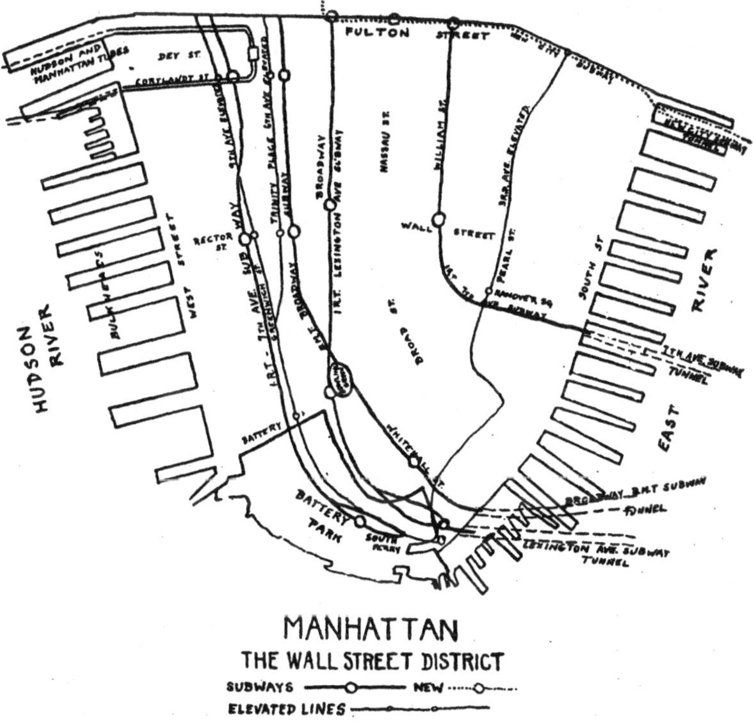

MANHATTAN

THE WALL STREET DISTRICT

SUBWAYS —o— NEW ····o····

ELEVATED LINES —•—•—

average rate of increase for the entire island during this period. The earlier years, during the boom which carried most real-estate values higher, indicate a more rapid rate of growth than was experienced in more recent times. In the eight years from 1905 to 1913, land in the vicinity rose in value by slightly more than 29 per cent whereas in the sixteen years following 1913, an additional gain of but 24 per cent was recorded.

Despite the fact that three new subway lines are now serving this area, and incidentally provide a greater number of transit stops than are to be found in any area of similar size in the City, land values have not experienced any very unusual growth.

As has been mentioned, the subway along Broadway had just been opened in 1905. The land within a one-block area on both sides of this new transit route had gained by 1913, 32.5 per cent over the values given for 1905. This is slightly more than the average gain of 29 per cent for the entire financial district during this period. However, this more rapid growth was seemingly short-lived, for since that date, this same area has experienced a rise in land values of only 17 per cent which brings the total gain for the quarter century to somewhat more than 55 per cent or less than the 60 per cent rise for the entire district.

The changes that have been witnessed along the routes of those subway lines which were constructed after 1913 are equally interesting. The West-side Seventh Avenue subway has an arm which, after leaving the main route, passes down William Street through Hanover Square and thence under the East River to Brooklyn. Contracts were let for this subway in 1913, and in 1918, service was begun. Land along either side of this subway registered a gain of 60 per cent for the period 1905-1924. Strangely enough, however, there is little evidence of any remarkable change in the rate of growth in values after the coming of the subway, for prior to 1913, a gain of 24 per cent was evidenced, while since that year, a 27 per cent jump has occurred in land values.

On the West side, two other subways were constructed: the Broadway (B.M.T.) subway, which in this section passes through Whitehall and Church Streets, and the other arm of the Seventh Avenue subway, which passes down Greenwich Street to South Ferry. The former was opened in 1915 and the latter in 1918. These subways are so closely situated that the land abutting on the one line, is also fronting on the other one. The value of the land in the area about these subways has shown a relatively higher rate of growth than is found for the complete section, averaging somewhat more than 80 per cent from 1905 to date. However, it is significant that prior to subway construction a rise of 39 per cent was evidenced while since 1913, the gain has been only 29.5 per cent.

While examining these shifts in land values in this financial district of Manhattan, it is also of interest to note that since 1921, the values of the land, except in isolated cases, have remained relatively stable. The average gains have fallen below 10 per cent for the period and in individual cases there have been slight declines from the 1921 level.

A striking feature of the financial district is that the land immediately adjacent to the subway and to the subway stations has not experienced any notable difference in value change from the general trend of change throughout the district. One reason for this is, perhaps, that the subway stations here do not create any individual centers of concentration. They are situated in such close proximity that they are within easy walking distance of each other. Furthermore, the transit arteries running north and south are spaced so that they are but one or two blocks apart. Therefore, it may be that any influence which they exert is spread throughout the whole district. It is indeed fortunate that the transit stops are so numerous that the large office population can be readily moved. Without them, the traffic congestion in the narrow streets here, would be unbearable. The fact remains, however, that since additional subways were built through this district, the rate of growth has been less rapid than before.

The more valuable sites lying in the heart of the financial district in the vicinity of Wall and Broad Streets and Broadway have not risen materially in value in recent years.

One explanation which has been offered for this condition

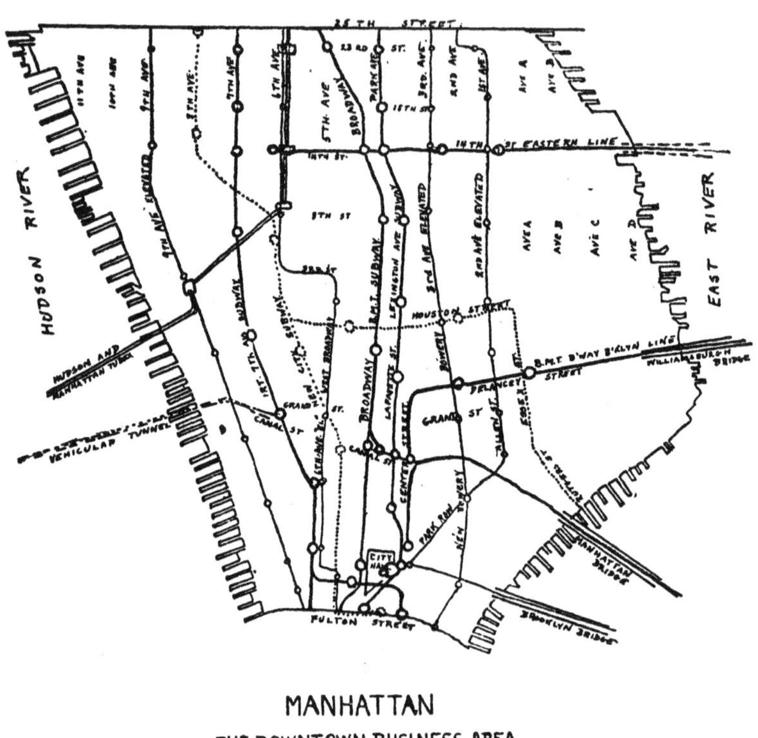

MANHATTAN

THE DOWNTOWN BUSINESS AREA

SUBWAYS — NEW ·········

ELEVATED LINES

HUDSON TUBES

is that many of these sites have reached their highest use (for the time being at least). Very large buildings of expensive construction tend to stabilize the values of their sites. If, of course, the demand for space in such vicinities runs ahead of building construction programs, the effect is to stimulate the site values of completed buildings. Where the space demands become insatiable in a built-up area in which little vacant land is to be had, the land values rise to such levels as to make it profitable to tear down existing structures in order to make way for new buildings of greater height. A stage is reached, at length, where it becomes economically undesirable to demolish existing structures. This occurs either when there is a surplus of rentable space or when cheaper sites may be obtained in the vicinity near the center of activity. This latter condition is evidenced in some of the rather large increases on Wall Street, in the direction of the East River. Several cases of this sort are observable, where the centralized plots remained comparatively stable, and a few lower-valued areas have made some appreciable gains. The extension of the financial area into adjacent territory which is less expensive and yet is within easy walking distance of the heart of the district, helps to explain the increasing demand for this land.

Although this district below Fulton Street showed a decline in the rate of growth in land value, it gained by much more than the average gains of the other lower portions of Manhattan. It has in its favor the existence of a more or less permanent nucleus of financial houses, stock and produce exchanges, and high-grade office buildings which tend to stabilize the land values which have been built up there. This tendency toward concentration is not on the wane, but rather on the increase. This is seen in the recent move of banks to build up a small banking community. Within a few blocks of one another, almost a dozen of the largest New York banks have leased space or started construction of large buildings to house their activities here. Nevertheless, it is apparent that the increased values which might be traceable to recent subway development in the financial district have been extremely moderate.

Passing to the district just above, up to 14th Street, a somewhat mottled effect is seen. This district, which represents approximately one-fifth of the area of Manhattan, can boast of having within its borders an arm of every transit artery serving the island. In 1905, four elevated lines were in this territory, with thirty-three stations, of which twelve were express stops. The East-side subway had also been opened, with seven stations. At that time, in the central core, bounded by the New Bowery, Bowery, and Third Avenue on the East, and by Hudson Street on the West, the blocks under observation had a land value of $260,738,000. With the exception of the stations on the Second and Ninth Avenue elevated lines, this central core includes all of the transit facilities serving this section.

In 1908-1909, the Hudson Tubes were opened at Christopher Street, 9th Street, and 14th Street. In 1913, the Center Street loop, connecting the bridges, was opened. In 1913, the land value had become $265,190,000—a growth of minute percentage, in view of the fact that there was more or less of a realty boom in Manhattan as a whole during this period. Evidently, property values did not seem to be awakened by these new transit lines. The older lines, too, seem to have lost their effect in stimulating growth in land values.

Upon examining the situation somewhat more closely, it will be seen that this change was not uniform over the whole length of this central core. From Fulton Street to Grand Street the land values showed a rise of about nine per cent over the 1905 values. The apparent lack of growth shown for the whole area is then clearly traceable to the land north of Grand Street. This is demonstrated by the fact that if the segment from Grand Street to 14th Street is taken by itself, a *decline* in land values of six per cent from 1905-1913 is discovered.

In 1915, the Center Street Loop had one new station added to it. In 1917, the Broadway B.M.T. subway was opened to 14th Street, thus adding four stations, one of which was an express stop. In 1920 this line was extended south of Canal Street, and contributed two more local stations and one express station. Meanwhile, in 1918, the new Seventh Avenue Subway line had been opened and thus provided seven more points of access. In 1924, the 14th Street-Eastern line was opened with three stations. Summarizing, this central area, running from Fulton Street to 14th Street, received from the year 1913 to 1929 eighteen additional transit stops along four different lines.

In 1929 the land value for this area was $264,615,000. From this it would appear that in a quarter century, this large section of Manhattan gained in value by no more than 1½ per cent. As a matter of fact, however, the situation is really worse.

Its significance is not fully appreciated until the area in question is still more closely analyzed. If each individual block is studied, it will be found that there is a scattering of increases of between 100 and 200 per cent in parts of this central core, especially in the vicinity of the Seventh Avenue subway and in certain zones south of Chambers Street. The inclusion of these blocks naturally raises the average in the calculations. When the land lying between Sixth and Third Avenues is separately considered, it is found that from 1905-1929 an average decline in value of over 10 per cent has been felt. This is the very center of downtown Manhattan. It has Broadway as its main artery. Both the Broadway subway and the Lexington Avenue subway have stations in it. The Sixth Avenue elevated, and part of the Seventh Avenue subway borders it on the West, and the Third Avenue elevated forms its eastern boundary. Transit arteries from three bridges run into it. The new subway under construction passes through it. In total, it includes fourteen elevated stations, and twenty-two subway stations plus four stations on the new line. Nevertheless, with all of these points in its favor, so far as accessibility is concerned, it has not succeeded in keeping pace with the growth of the rest of the island, but has slid backward to below its value of a quarter century ago.

What happened in the areas outside this central core, between the same north and south boundaries, within the same period? On the East Side, the only transit line in 1905 was the elevated system along First Avenue, and the Third Avenue line which bounded its western border. The two stations of Essex Street and Bowery, on the B. M. T. Williamsburgh Bridge line, and the two stations on the 14th Street-Eastern line on its northern border, were the only additions in transit facilities made since that time. From 1905-1913, this area showed an average increase in land value of 23 per cent—the more southerly sections showing a smaller rate of increase than those further north. South of Grand Street, the gain was 16 per cent; north of that street, the advance was about 26 per cent. From 1913-1929, this area resembled the central core in declining in land value by from 18 to 20 per cent throughout its length. On the West side, the one and only line existing in 1905 was the Ninth Avenue elevated system. This ran along Greenwich Street. No changes have been made in transit since that time in this region, save the fact that it is not very far from the Seventh Avenue Subway, constructed in 1918. From 1905 to 1913, land values rose by 21 per cent. Between 1913-1929, they practically remained stationary. How may these rather surprising land-value changes be accounted for?

This large downtown region, unlike the Wall Street District, has seen shifts of many kinds. New York has often been called the "City of Unrest". This part of the city at least, testifies to the truth of this statement. It has witnessed the coming and passing of the fine residential areas around Washington Square, the many changes in the Greenwich Village section, the shifts of shopping districts, theater districts, and the northward movement of trades, wholesale houses, and business offices. Such has been the history of this region, and it has been closely reflected in the land values.

Directly north of Fulton Street, most of the lofty buildings and warehouses, as well as office buildings and tenements were fairly well filled with tenants prior to 1913, and land values rose. However, a movement northward, and over the bridges to Brooklyn and Queens, began about this time, in order to take advantage of lower rentals and better quarters elsewhere. The continued decline since 1913 in the central core just north of Fulton Street is partly explained by the fact that the Grand Central Zone is drawing part of the office tenantry from this area. The strength of this movement did not become so great until recent years, since which time tremendous building activity has been going on in the midtown section. This accounts for the fact that this downtown office section still experienced a growth in value until 1913. A noticeable decline has been witnessed since.

It will be recalled, however, that the earliest and most severe declines came north of Chambers Street. In 1904, when the first subway was opened on Fourth Avenue, a movement uptown in real estate demands had already begun to manifest itself. Residences had become more popular in more northerly sections of Manhattan, and the few important retail stores which still remained, were leasing new quarters in the 34th and 42nd Street areas. Furthermore, the silk business, which had contributed an important class of tenants in this region, shifted north in 1907. Prominent real-estate brokers, familiar with the district, state that high insurance rates were partly responsible for this shift. The San Francisco fire and earthquake the preceding year, had caused great losses to insurance companies all over the country, and as a result, insurance rates were generally raised by about 25 per cent. The older buildings housing the silk industry were great fire risks, and the insurance was made unbearably heavy. A set of fireproof, sprinkler-type buildings were erected between 14th and 23rd Street, having relatively lower rentals because of larger space facilities and enjoying lower insurance rates. The silk trades were quick to adopt these quarters, and were followed by other concerns in rapid order, who desired to move to the more modern buildings in this newer area.

A gradual movement had started northward among the manufacturers of men's wear, who desired to enter "a more favorable marketing district." The women's garment industry was evidencing an even more noticeable shift. At one time located entirely south of 14th Street, it was already moving to 23rd Street in the beginning of the Century. By 1917, the movement had carried itself to 38th Street, and had swung mainly to the west of Fifth Avenue. Since then, the development of the Garment Center west of Seventh Avenue, between 34th and 39th Streets has occurred. This was somewhat artificially secured through the attempt of the Save New York Committee "to preserve Fifth Avenue as a retail district."

The wholesale markets must establish themselves in close proximity to the retail stores, so as to be advantageously placed for the buyers of those stores. Consequently, a northward trend was experienced in these groups, when the department stores began to move uptown. Especially was this true in the cases of clothing, textiles, and furs. At the opening of the Twentieth Century, all of the wholesale groups were established below 14th Street; the majority are now to be found above 23rd Street. This is also partly explained by the fact that out-of-town buyers are more easily catered to in the midtown section with its hotel and terminal facilities.

The East Side area, it will be recalled, showed a tendency to increase in land value up to 1913, despite its failure to get more transit. The greater part of this area houses the bulk of the contractors' plants in the men's wear industry, and is also the residential site for most of the workers of the industry, who live in Manhattan. From the beginning of the Twentieth Century, until the War, these plants were on the increase. During and after the war a noticeable number of the plants shifted to other boroughs. The migration of workers to new residential locations was also a feature of this movement. The cost of living was rising during the War, and the high New York rents made it inviting for people to leave this area whenever possible. In an article dated October, 1926, Edward M. Law of the Board of Transportation of New York City states that the very dense population of the lower East Side had been decreasing at the rate of about 10,000 per year in the last five years. While this locality still holds the leadership in this industry in Manhattan, its position is a declining one, rather than one of growth. Moreover, the tendency of this trade to use buildings of an obsolete nature and at lower rentals has prevented the land values from rising materially.

In one of the reports published in the *Regional Plan of New York and its Environs* [1] appears the following: . . .

New York's transportation system has enabled a large part of the processes of fabricating and merchandising to concentrate near the shopping district in Manhattan and to follow its movements at short notice, and by frequent steps (from below

[1] *Regional Plan of New York and its Environs*, Economic and Industrial Survey, The Clothing and Textile Industries, Selekman, Walter and Couper, pp. 19-20.

Fourteenth Street to its present location) without losing touch with a huge labor pool. In earlier times the industries seem to have been located to a considerable extent with reference to the homes of the workers in the old ghetto. But with the transportation developments of the last twenty years no less than 40 per cent of the women's garment workers now employed on Manhattan Island have gone to live in the boroughs of Brooklyn and the Bronx, whence they travel daily to the Manhattan workshops (53,000 persons). From 15,000 to 16,000 (garment) workers travel daily from upper to lower Manhattan.

This has a double significance. It means that the subways are actually facilitating the movement of industries from place to place in Manhattan, and at the same time act to make possible a residential shift on the part of the workers in those industries. Where a definite movement is already under way for a change in location, the subway may accelerate the change rather than retard it. The influence upon land values in the district experiencing this drain in tenantry is not likely to be a desirable one.

Delancey Street has practically doubled in land value since 1913. It might be suggested that the B.M.T. line coming over the Williamsburgh Bridge caused this increase. It will be found, however, that Delancey Street was the only street to show a gain—all adjoining territory, even that surrounding Essex Street and Bowery stations, showed little growth in value and some of the land experienced a loss. It is also noteworthy that this line was opened in 1913, and that no appreciable gains were witnessed along Delancey Street until after 1925. The occasion for this doubling of values is rather to be found in the construction of the Schiff Parkway along Delancey Street after 1925, as an approach to the Bridge.

Another interesting case of land-value growth in this area which has shown an average loss is that of Avenue A.

Above the tenements and push-carts of this East Side region, are rising up-to-date apartment houses, with roof gardens to add brilliance to the otherwise unattractive section — save for its own exotic local coloring. Advance leasing in these apartments is going well, and several more buildings of this type are planned. The nearest transit line is the Second Avenue elevated, which has been standing for decades. The nearest subway station is fully seven blocks distant—and this does not provide through service in Manhattan without requiring a change of trains two stations beyond. Yet, values have risen from two per cent to 25 per cent along here since 1913, the greater part of this growth coming in the last two years. Evidently the subways have little to do with this change.

Since 1913, the land along Lafayette Street has declined in value, despite the fact that the Lexington Avenue subway has five stations along its route on this street. In the same way, land along the Center Street route has declined. Similarly, a drop of 2½ per cent has been witnessed north of City Hall Park, along the Broadway subway. The forces operating for a decline in land values have evidently been more powerful than any stimulus which the subways might have provided.

The Seventh Avenue subway passed through a different experience. During the first few years of its construction, up to the time of its opening (1918), every parcel of land along its route showed a decline in value. Then in 1920, land along Varick Street rose in value, and by 1924, the land on West Broadway from Park Place to Reade Streets had also risen. By 1928, land on Varick Street was worth more than double its 1915 value. The building of the Varick Street extension, connecting Varick Street with Seventh Avenue, and the creation of a new wide artery from Franklin to 14th Street by this operation, should not be overlooked, however, in studying this growth in values. The lower part of this area, moreover, is also located at the Plaza for the Vehicular tunnel. Many new business and commercial buildings have been erected here in the last few years. Entire blocks have been transformed. Not over a decade ago, there were still standing the old tenements and warehouses, and unattractive rows of small buildings, which now remain in a few scattered areas as reminders of a rapidly disappearing regime. Today, there have been erected in their place, large office and industrial buildings mostly in white brick and stone, and designed in accordance with the changed demands of modern business. Since 1925, over 10,000,000 square feet of floor space have been added to this district.

The remarkable feature of this district has been the almost perfect rental record of the new buildings. According to one of the prominent brokerage firms working in this vicinity, the demand for space in the structures now going up indicates that the new buildings will be as successful as regards leasing, as their predecessors have been.

The main reason given for the success of the developments is that here could be found about the only block fronts in Manhattan available for such improvements with convenient shipping and rail facilities, and with a subway running directly underneath.

The cheapness of the property as compared with sites located nearer the central zone and the increased demand for such property, naturally helped to send up values in this locality. It was not, however, until the hand of the realty operator and builder swept over this zone in search of profitable investments, that the demand for space was stimulated. The presence of the subway and of the vehicular tunnel plaza facilitated the success of their ventures.

The northern end of Varick Street is part of Greenwich Village. This was at one time the residential area of some of the most prominent of New York families. It was then deserted, deteriorating gradually, and ultimately became the refuge for artists and writers. Once again it took on a change and became a haven for those enjoying pseudo-Bohemian life. Recently, the tendency has been for a powerful drive in the direction of reconverting the whole area into an expensive, modern residential district. It took courage for the pioneers in this development to pour millions of dollars into apartment house projects in this community. Once successful, it did not take long to attract others. These changes have been rapidly reflected in the shifting values of this little section, quite regardless of any changes in transit facilities.

The latest development in transit to be made in the downtown business area is the Eighth Avenue subway, now being constructed. It may be interesting to note what is happening along the route of this transit artery prior to its opening. Construction work has been going on for the last three or four years. In 1922, the plans for the subway were not yet known. From 1922 to 1926, no striking changes had taken place in land values from the East River, along Fulton Street, and up to Church Street to Canal Street. No noticeable changes have taken place since, on Fulton Street. On Church Street, gains of as much as 25 per cent were recorded from Barclay Street to Worth Street, from 1926-1928. A subway station designed for Park Place, and one at Lispenard Street, have not yet stimulated any great rise in the value of land in the vicinity. From Canal Street, north, the subway takes a course along the Sixth Avenue extension—a new artery which will be a main thoroughfare connecting traffic from the Holland Tunnel and Manhattan Bridge through Canal Street, and uptown along Sixth Avenue. When the widening of Church Street is fully completed, a highway running from Battery Park to Central

Park will be ready. This extension which was made during 1928, necessitated the cutting through of ten blocks of old buildings. Values have already begun to rise through here. The future trend of values is unknown. The property owners here are being assessed for the street improvement. Should they be assessed for the subway which runs beneath the street? How much does the property benefit from each?

So far as outward appearances are concerned, life in this part of the new subway's path is still about the same. It is probably too early to judge the effects, for the area has not yet come completely out of the construction stage. South of 14th Street, wooden streets still indicate that the work below the surface is not quite completed. Comparing this section along its route, however, with those further north, the contrast is rather striking. There have been some impressive changes in the midtown zone. But up to the last little wooden cottage at 14th Street, which has stamped this area as a district of modest homes since the Colonial days, " it is still the Village, brooding and slow to change."

The other route of the new subway in this district, along Rutgers, Essex, and Houston Streets, gives evidence of a gain along fifteen blocks, while nineteen blocks have not changed materially in land value since 1922. There seems to be little uniformity in the influence of the new subway through this area. What ultimate results are to be found in land-value changes throughout this region, the future alone can show. For the present, however, its career can be said to have been extremely spotty, with a strong tendency downward, rather than an upward movement in land values. Indeed, transit facilities offered little relief from this monotony of decline, and any influences which may be attributed to them, have been extremely varied in character.

The region from 14th Street to 25th Street has passed through much the same history. It was thought best to separate it from the other downtown business area in this study, so as to show clearly how it was affected by the northward shift coming from below and moving through it to regions further uptown. In 1905 four elevated lines and one subway ran through here from north to south. In 1909, the Hudson tunnels were extended northward through this area, and in 1918, two new subway lines were opened—also running north and south. The 14th Street-Eastern line on the southern border of this district, running easterly from Sixth Avenue, was opened in 1924.

As was to be expected from an acquaintance with the northerly movements in real estate demands which were taking place in the South of the island, land values rose throughout this region from 1905 to 1913. The gains ranged from six per cent to 90 per cent for portions of the section, the greatest increases occurring east of Broadway. Here the average gains were 50 per cent. This was the area served by the new subway of 1904. Here were located the new fireproof buildings that had helped to attract the trades to Fourth and Fifth Avenues above 14th Street. Far-sighted builders had evidently chosen the sites for their buildings along the subway route. Had the subway passed through another avenue, would land values have behaved differently? What would have occurred if these lofts had been built on Seventh Avenue instead of on Fourth and Fifth Avenues?

A subway was built on Seventh Avenue, and the erection of loft buildings in that area had taken place by the time the subway was opened in 1918. An average increase of 80 per cent occurred in land values in the region running two blocks west of Seventh Avenue between the time that construction work was started on the subway, and 1929. The same area gained by only seven per cent between 1905-1913—the same period during which the property along the other subway route had mounted 50 per cent. Of course, only one block to the East, was the Sixth Avenue elevated, and two blocks to the West, was the Ninth Avenue elevated line, but nevertheless some degree of accessibility was added by the subway, for these blocks are comparatively long. The important point to remember, however, is that new loft buildings in this area were attracting tenants and that the subway was therefore passing through an area actively in demand. It should not be forgotten that a decline in land values occurred along this same subway, and during the same period of time, in the lower section of Manhattan between Reade and Franklin Streets.

On the extreme West side, outside of the central core, between Ninth and Tenth Avenues and on the northern fringe of this downtown district, some record progress is being made at present in converting the old Chelsea area into what is considered to be the world's largest apartment development. Here too, the land values have made gains similar to those just cited for the district immediately east of this area. Although the buildings are still in the course of construction, and the first units are not scheduled to be ready until May, 1930, it is reported that two of these units between 23rd and 24th Streets are already over fifty per cent leased. The new subway will pass along Eighth Avenue—one block from here, sometime in 1931. In the meantime however, space is already greatly in demand. The Ninth Avenue elevated line, the crosstown trolley connecting with the Seventh Avenue, the Broadway, and the Lexington Avenue subways, and taxi service, make this development quite accessible at present. Moroever, the units are expected to be so complete in themselves, with every urban need provided for, that they will form a veritable apartment city. Naturally, with this amazing change which has suddenly swept over this old district, which for years showed little sign of growth, land values have rapidly advanced—reflecting these new demands for space.

Like the Seventh Avenue subway, the Broadway B.M.T. subway was also opened in 1918. What happened to the land values between the Seventh Avenue and the Broadway subways since 1913? They declined! The land there today is worth less than it was in 1905. A drop of over 30 per cent has taken place since its high value of 1911 was reached. In fact, the whole central area between the Seventh Avenue subway and the Fourth Avenue line, dropped in land value by as much as 23 to 28 per cent in this period! What occurred here? Does the Seventh Avenue subway affect property east of it differently than property west of it? Haven't these subways exerted their influences as yet? Can it be said that they have been important in keeping up land values; that values would have dropped still more had it not been for the subway? Perhaps, but this would be the vainest theory and would offer little consolation to the landowner.

Even before any new subways were built in this area, land was beginning to lose its favor. Prospects of future growth of the City, had induced some of the leading stores in the 23rd Street retail section, to move further uptown. Furthermore, with the establishment of the needle trades in the vicinity of the shopping district, the throngs of workers thrown upon the streets in the noon-hour lunch period threatened the accessibility of patrons to the stores. In order to escape the street traffic congestion many of the stores were prompted to move uptown. Therefore, although land was still in demand in this vicinity, the gradual removal of the department stores and specialty shops prevented as rapid a rise as would otherwise have probably occurred. Since retail shopping centers are regarded as one of the highest uses to which real estate can be put, this section was actually falling from a higher to a lower use. Following

1913, this became even more noticeable, for the midtown district began to draw away most of the important tenants from this lower area.

Between Fourth and Second Avenues, the land increased in value by 28 per cent following 1913. Yet this gain for a sixteen year period is small when compared with the increase of 50 per cent for this strip over a previous and shorter period. As has already been noticed, the land directly west of this subway has shown appreciable declines in value. How long does the influence of the subway last? Does the greater part of the increased value arise immediately upon the opening of the subway, and then taper off? May the increased value be delayed in coming for many years? Does the effect vary under different circumstances?

The latter suggestion comes nearest the truth in the light of the experience in Manhattan. If this is so, what are the circumstances that are conducive to the occurrence of a value increase? Does the problem not really resolve itself into a "subway-plus" concept?

In studying the influences of subways on land values it must be remembered that many other factors must enter into the story. To compare land values with the extension of subway routes without recognizing these other factors, is to attempt to establish a false correlation. The value of land depends upon how much a certain locality is in demand, and for what uses such land is to be put. Increase in accessibility to land otherwise undesirable for certain purposes may have little effect upon its value. Where increased accessibility enhances the desirability of areas which already appear promising, the value is likely to increase materially.

CHAPTER V

The Midtown District

In the whole midtown section, land values have steadily advanced since 1905. When the first subway was opened in 1904, the retail stores were already moving to 34th Street. Macy's, for example, established themselves at 34th Street in 1902. They were soon followed by other department stores and specialty shops. The 23rd Street Center had been the retail shopping district and the important stores were located on Sixth Avenue and Broadway. The location of the Macy store was chosen in all probability in anticipation of the Pennsylvania terminal which was to be erected one block from the site. The rest of the movement proceeded along Broadway and Fifth Avenue. The opening of the new subways, the announcement of the location of the Pennsylvania Station, and the extension of the Hudson Tubes to 33rd Street stimulated the northward march. The construction of new transit lines within this area came at a time when they added impetus to a movement already in progress. The result of this is shown in the tremendous rise in land values along some of these subway routes.

Anticipation in this territory was nevertheless stronger than actual achievement, at first. This accounts for the less rapid rate of growth here shortly after 1913 as compared with the rate of growth in land values prior to that year. On this point, Mr. Lawson Purdy said in 1917:[1]

[1] *Proceedings of the Ninth National Conference on City Planning,* Kansas City, May 7-9, 1917, pp. 236-241.

When Pennsylvania Station was planned and built there was a great land boom at that point. Values rose to very high speculative figures—far higher than the land was worth at that time, all through that section. The station took a good while to build and open, and it was a disappointment to the Pennsylvania Railroad at the time. It took time to develop the traffic East to Long Island, partly because the subway that was expected to run up Seventh Avenue took a long time to build. The value of land in this territory as shown by sales, was not borne out in use up to 1917. Ultimately the values will sometime reach the economic values that sales indicated in 1912-13.

The Pennsylvania terminal was not completed until 1910. The Seventh Avenue subway which was to connect with it, was not opened until 1918. The Fourth Avenue subway which had been opened in 1904 therefore tended to draw this northward tide further toward the East of the island. Development of this side of Manhattan had been furthered by the arrivals daily, of the large commuting population from Long Island City via the Ferry to 34th Street. It is estimated that in 1905, the 34th Street spur from the Second and Third Avenue elevated lines to the Ferry carried over 20,000,000 passengers annually. From 1905-1913 the land in the central core east of Broadway and Sixth Avenue, as far north as 40th Street rose in value by over 55 per cent. Between Broadway and Park Avenue the average gains were as high as 75 per cent. The land to the West gained by a trifle under 50 per cent; although individual lots around the Pennsylvania Station averaged much higher. Following 1913, the western half of this section became the focal point for an ever-increasing commuting and traveling population arriving in New York. Like a magnet, it drew large hotels, office buildings and stores into its territory. Furthermore, the famous controversy over location for the women's wear industry was finally concluded around 1916, when the Garment Center Capitol was built west of Seventh Avenue, between 34th and 39th Streets. Values then rose over 100

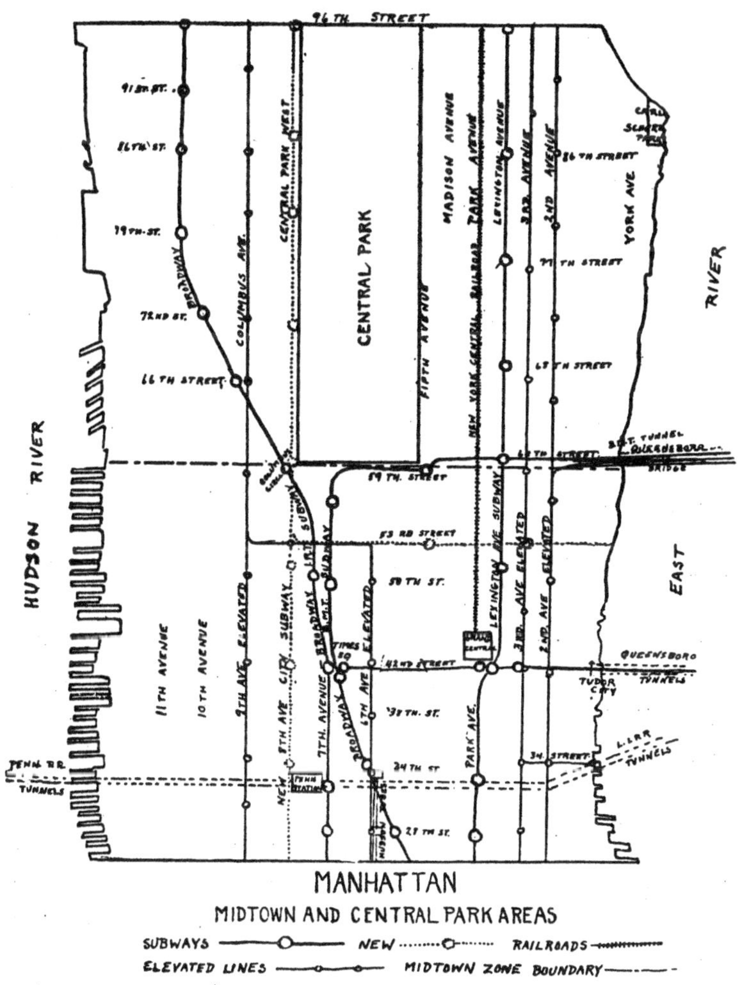

MANHATTAN
MIDTOWN AND CENTRAL PARK AREAS

SUBWAYS — NEW ······ RAILROADS
ELEVATED LINES — MIDTOWN ZONE BOUNDARY

per cent between 1913 and 1929. The greater part of this rise took place, however, in the years following the war. Up to 1921, the gain in land values was nine per cent. In the eight years following that year there has been experienced a growth amounting to more than 80 per cent.

The eastern half of the section also showed an increase over 40 per cent, but the later history of this section has shown a less rapid growth than was witnessed before the expansion of the western part. There has been an important swing from East to West here. A crosstown subway from Seventh Avenue to Fourth Avenue at 34th Street would probably work materially toward " ironing out " the differences in rates of growth of the East and West Sides in this area. The conversion of the 33rd Street Station on the Fourth Avenue line into an express stop, would probably benefit the eastern area.

The extreme East side of 34th Street, presents an interesting problem. From Third Avenue to the East River is the elevated railroad spur which connects the Second and Third Avenue elevated lines with the Long Island City Ferry. It will be recalled that this was referred to as one of the sources of stimulus to the growth of this section around 1905. Today it has outlived its use. The Pennsylvania tunnels and the Queensboro subway lines take care of the Long Island crowds coming into the midtown section. The drift of business has gone further west. The result has been to make this part of 34th Street stagnant, while all the rest of it enjoys rapid progress. It is felt that this area is now ready for improvement with modern apartment houses and office buildings. Several new buildings, including apartments and hotels are already contemplated. Cold water tenements and antiquated loft buildings now occupying the sites are being removed to be replaced with modern improvements. The property owners and merchants of the 34th Street Midtown Association have formulated a petition for the removal of the spur. A quotation from the petition reads:

The elevated structure is obsolete. The service rendered is too slow for rapid transit. It is seldom used by passengers so that no loss to the railroad is incurred. The existence of the structure is a detriment to the property facing it, and it is an impediment to the healthy growth of the neighborhood immediately surrounding it.

A number of operators have been buying land in this vicinity in anticipation of reaping the gains in value which it is estimated will result if efforts of these petitioning groups are successful. By way of further illustration of the present attitude toward the influence of some of the existing elevated structures in Manhattan upon the value of abutting property, it is of interest to note that for a large plot facing the Third Avenue elevated structure, a lease has recently been closed, in which there is specifically provided that the tenant will pay a substantially increased rental for the premises if during the life of the lease, the elevated structure is removed. This is believed to be the first time that a clause of this nature has been embodied in a lease.

In the very center of this part of the midtown zone south of 40th Street, the fashionable Murray Hill district, between Third and Sixth Avenues, which had early become one of the most exclusive residential areas, housing the Astors, Havemeyers, Sims, Morgans, Bakers, Wendells and Pynes, was threatened on all sides by the onrush uptown which the Twentieth Century witnessed. One by one, the fringes of this district gave way, and stately mansions were replaced by modern sky-scrapers. The famous iron-bound Murray Hill agreement of 1847 in which this district was restricted as a residential area, has withstood the onward march of trade and commerce, however, and today this little area hemmed in by tall buildings surrounding it, still tries to maintain much of its residential character. The desirability of the land for commercial purposes is so great that land values have risen to astonishing levels, levels so high, in fact, that a prominent real-estate promoter is quoted as saying that the maintenance cost of a residence there "represents an extravagance which even the most wealthy will consider prohibitive." Just on the northern fringe of this strip, is the spot which some authorities concede to be New York's most valuable land.

In 1905, the only subway line from 40th to 59th Streets was the shuttle from Fourth Avenue and 42nd Street, over to Times Square, and thence north along Broadway. The same four elevated lines coming from downtown continued their course through this section from 40th to 59th Street. The heart of this area north of 40th Street, and from Ninth Avenue on the West, to Third Avenue on the East, gained over 35 per cent before 1913, and slightly more than 130 per cent since that time. Values continued to rise throughout the war period, whereas a decrease was experienced in most of the other parts of the island. The figures cited above are for comparatively large stretches of land. They do not speak for individual parcels. In the vicinity of Grand Central Station and of Times Square, for example, land values increased by several hundred per cent. As the distance from these two centers increases, values taper off rapidly.

If the central core of this section is divided in half at Sixth Avenue, the Times Square area shows the greater growth in value over the Grand Central area. The former increased 46 per cent up to 1913, and 140 per cent since then; the latter showed a gain of 28 per cent during the first period, and 125 per cent in the second period. Both have received subway extensions since 1913. The eastern half was given the new Lexington Avenue subway north of 42nd Street in 1918; the western half received the new Broadway B.M.T. subway along Seventh Avenue north of 42nd Street, in 1918 and 1920. In both cases, the largest part of the gains in value came after 1921.

The greatest stimulus which the eastern side received was the improvement of the Grand Central area which was started in 1903 and completed in 1913. The New York Central railroad had formerly maintained open railway yards north of the station up to 51st Street. Then, as far as 96th Street, the steam engines ran underground, but open vents were placed all along Park Avenue for the escape of steam and smoke. This situation created an undesirable environment for any high-class development, and as a result, cheap residences and manufacturing establishments, breweries, etc., were lined up along the route. Under its improvement project, the New York Central covered the open cut, created new cross streets north of 45th Street, and electrified its lines, which made possible the elimination of the vents, and the creation of a beautiful wide road along Park Avenue. The effect was magical. The New York Central itself built new buildings within the newly created blocks, and many hotels, and office structures were quick to follow. North of the terminal, up to 59th Street, land values increased by more than 200 per cent since 1914, along Park Avenue. The growth of this avenue had not been appreciable before that date. Mr. Lawson Purdy, speaking about this region at a conference held in 1917 [1] said: " So long as the railroad was operated by coal engines, I cannot say that there could have been any large increment of value on that avenue. There might have been some, there doubtless would have been, but there would have been no such development as we now have on that avenue." A widening of the roadway of Park Avenue which has been taking place during the last few years has further contributed to its attractiveness.

Lexington Avenue, now served by the subway, showed

[1] *Proceedings of the Ninth National Conference on City Planning*, Kansas City, May 7-9, 1917. The electrification of the N. Y. Central, and Effect on Property Values, Lawson Purdy.

some phenomenal changes, and small shacks were soon replaced by loft and office buildings. Stores came to be heavily in demand, especially in the vicinity of the terminal, and business property boomed. The land in this vicinity showed a slight tendency to anticipate the opening of the new subway, although all of this area was affected in value by the New York Central improvement. From 1911, when construction work began, to 1918, when the subway was opened, land values showed increases in a range from less than one per cent to 59 per cent along Lexington Avenue. In the ten years since that time, the advance in values has been between 150 per cent and 300 per cent on the average. This street is still enjoying an expansion which is marked by great building activity. There has been during the past few years, very extensive buying north of 42nd Street, and many large plots have been accumulated by business interests and realty syndicates. The greater part of the area will eventually be improved with tall office buildings each covering several thousand square feet. A great part of the recent buying and planning ahead is ascribed to the feeling among realty interests that the time is not far distant when the application to rezone Park Avenue below 59th Street to the New York Central Building for retail trade and commercial office use will be granted. The new Chrysler Building, the Graybar Building, and the Chanin Building are conspicuous examples of the trend of realty development along this thoroughfare. The new Waldorf Astoria, on Lexington Avenue and 50th Street marks the nucleus of a new hotel center which is developing in the upper regions of Lexington Avenue, where some half dozen hotels have been erected within the past few years.

Equally startling from the standpoint of rapidly changing land values have been the careers of Madison and Fifth Avenues in this district. Fifth Avenue became the most fashionable retail shopping area of New York. Madison Avenue rapidly developed large building construction. The Fifth Avenue shopping area has continued to creep northward until the predictions that Fifth Avenue in the neighborhood of 57th and 59th Streets was destined to be a great retail and office center have already been fulfilled. But the movement has proceeded beyond, for 57th Street which has been the site for fine private homes, has also yielded to the relentless business expansion and has become a cross-town thoroughfare for exclusive specialty shops, between Fifth and Lexington Avenues and 59th Street is now following the same course. Evidences of this are already seen in the building of specialty shops in the street floors of the hotels in this vicinity, the construction of a ten-story office and store building on 59th Street and Madison Avenue, and in the expansion in size of the big Bloomingdale store at 59th Street.

The convenience of the offices to commuters coming into Grand Central made office structures very popular in this zone, and helped to drain some of the tenants from the downtown office districts.

Mr. Frank W. Crane in an article on this subject, shows that the competition between what has been called the " Little Wall Street " uptown, (owing to the large banking and financial interests in the Grand Central Zone), and the established downtown financial district, is growing keener and that there is a tendency not only to duplicate these downtown values in this midtown center, but to exceed them.

Store sites have also increased in demand here. According to a recent survey made by the Loring M. Hewen Company, Inc., chain stores are more strongly entrenched in the Grand Central zone than in any other section of the City. Of the available ground-floor business locations in the heart of the Grand Central section, over 50 per cent of them are said to be occupied by chain stores, and this report concludes that although a great many business locations are coming into the market through the erection of new buildings, the demand for chain-store space in this zone still exceeds the supply. " Virtually every kind of retail business that figures in chain operation is represented in the Grand Central zone, from doughnut shops to banks."

The building of the B. M. T. subway in 1920, which made Seventh Avenue below 59th Street readily accessible to residents of Queens made for a still greater popularization of the midtown district. Further, inasmuch as the existence of Central Park prevented the expansion of business northward, without separating East from West, and because the two big railway terminals brought such large crowds into the midtown district, this area has shown a greater rise in value within the last generation than any other section of Manhattan.

When Frederick Brown, well-known real estate operator was recently interviewed and asked to select the ten most valuable sites in the city, he selected the following:

Broadway and Wall Street
Broad and Wall Street
Fifth Avenue and Forty-second Street
Broadway and Forty-second Street
Fifth Avenue and Fifty-seventh Street
Madison Avenue and Forty-second Street
Lexington Avenue and Forty-second Street
Broadway and Thirty-fourth Street
Madison Avenue and Fifty-ninth Street
Park Avenue and Fifty-ninth Street

While there may be some divergence of opinion among real estate men on this subject, it is noteworthy that in the selection of this authority, eight out of the ten sites mentioned are in the midtown area.

The movement uptown along Broadway created a diagonal stream from East to West. The theatrical interests that had held their posts for so long around 23rd and 14th Streets were one of the first groups to move into the Forties. By the end of the Nineteenth Century, 42nd Street had become the established theatrical center. One after another, Broadway and the side streets running east and west of it, filled up with theaters, first up to the Fifties, and later even up to Columbus Circle. Moreover, retail stores were beginning to take advantage of the transient traffic passing through this district. The establishment of Times Square as a meeting place for three subway lines accelerated this growth. Hotels and office buildings followed, and more recently, combination theater and office structures. The wide connecting link of 42nd Street between the valuable growing sections of East and West, became the site for many stores and offices. Respecting this theater area, Mr. Adolph Zukor said in 1926;[1]

> First, the centering of the motion picture theaters in this section has caused a fabulous increase in property values. In almost every instance the building of a motion picture theater caused the demolition of old buildings which have outlived their usefulness. The result was that not only was the value of the property largely increased, but the effect was felt on surrounding lands. . . . But the opening of the Strand, and other houses that have been built since, with their moderate prices, prices within the reach of all, brought to Broadway hundreds of thousands of people who before that time had found their amusement elsewhere.

The demand justified the raising of rents. Without the subways, the great throngs could not have been brought to the theaters. Without the theaters, the need of the subways in

[1] Broadway, the Grand Canyon of American Business, Broadway Association, New York, 1926, Influence of the Motion Picture, A. Zukor, p. 110.

this area might not have become so acute. Theatrical houses and music halls which could no longer afford to pay the high rentals that were resulting, were forced to move further uptown.

A comparison of the areas between Ninth Avenue and the Hudson River, and Third Avenue and the East River in this section is interesting. From 1905 to 1913 both of these properties displayed like characteristics. Both followed the central core in rising, but both characteristically rose by less than the central core. On the West Side, the increase was 30 per cent. On the East Side it was 17 per cent. The West Side had the advantage of being in closer contact with incoming and outgoing trade at the piers, and property available for lofts and warehouses was valuable. The East Side was equipped with greater numbers of cold water tenements, and cheap dwellings and near the River's edge were the ill-smelling abattoirs. Subway facilities were lacking in both areas. Both were served by elevated lines. From 1913-1929, the West Side values increased by 93 per cent; the East Side by 200 per cent. What caused this change? The growth on the West Side can be explained by the fact that the demand for space in the high-priced Times Square territory forced a shift further West; moreover the new Eighth Avenue subway has stimulated interest in this district. A story lies behind the exceptional East Side rise.

The whim of some of the society leaders in selecting the Sutton Place site, between 57th and 59th Streets, along the East River as a residential district for the well-to-do, started apartment-house construction there, and brought millions to owners of property. Some of the residents of the Park Avenue section, notably Mrs. Vanderbilt, became tired of this high-class residential street, and decided to erect stately mansions on the cheaper East Side, and at a fraction of the high Park Avenue overhead. This residential shift attracted others of the same social circle, and soon a great demand developed for this land. A rapid increase in land values resulted. Also, the operations of Fred French in buying out the cheap, unattractive land near the waterfront on the East River, and converting it into a high-class apartment development known as Tudor City, extending north of 42nd Street, are responsible for a phenomenal rise of land values here. One of the advertised merits of the development is that it makes it possible for many people to live within walking distance from their work in the midtown district. In this expansion then, the subway had little influence.

Another feature of this 42nd Street district on the East Side is the removal of the elevated spur which ran from Third avenue to Grand Central Station. This was removed in 1924. In a pamphlet issued by the Borough President of Manhattan in 1928, the following statement occurs [1]:

> Only partly used, the railroad structure was an obstruction not only to traffic, but to the progress of the most important crosstown street in the City, and its removal after years of agitation was in the nature of a transformation. At that point today, it would be hard to recognize the Forty-second Street of a few years ago. The result was phenomenal, and started a progressive movement that is rapidly extending to the East River.

From 1923 to 1928, this land multiplied in value by four or five times. A similar case to that just cited was the removal of the elevated spur on Sixth Avenue and 53rd to 59th Streets, and the widening of the roadway. Here again, land values soared.

One thing more remains for observation in this midtown area; namely, the behavior of land values along the new

[1] *Public Improvements in Manhattan*, Julius Miller, President, Borough of Manhattan, 1928, p. 27.

Eighth Avenue subway route. Since the Fall of 1924, when Eighth Avenue came to be pretty definitely known as the site selected for the new line, values have tended to increase in this section, especially north of 35th Street. Gains have ranged on an average of 80 per cent from 25th to 59th Streets, whereas this same land increased by only 44 per cent from 1909 to 1924.

Upon examining the present condition of the neighborhood through which this new subway is being constructed, quite a different view is presented than that which was witnessed further downtown. Close to 30th Street, rises the avenue's first giant setback skyscraper, and from here to Columbus Circle, the skyline is impressive. The Pennsylvania station as well as the U. S. Post Office are already established, and lend dignity to the Thirties. Banks and hotels are being constructed.

Mr. James W. Danahy of the Eighth Avenue Association, recently made a report in which he summarized the progress which has been made in this area. He pointed out that the district has become a hotel center in a short time with the building of a group of skyscraper hotels on Eighth Avenue near Times Square. He furthermore indicated that ten banks have established headquarters in Eighth Avenue in the past four years. The spread of theaters and of office buildings north of 42nd Street is also being watched. New stores with new fronts are rapidly taking the place of the older, dilapidated structures.

A recent newspaper article (*New York Times,* February 2, 1930), after commenting upon the motley character of the Eighth Avenue district further down-town, correctly expresses the significance of the changes which seem to have accompanied the construction of the new subway in this mid-town area as follows:

Here Eighth Avenue comes abruptly abreast of the flourishing times of other avenues in the midtown sections. Tall buildings . . . jut into the air; at night, lights blaze from a haphazard array of spacious windows; and on the sidewalks are bright store fronts. Further up, the avenue again assumes a more nondescript character.

Through this area, then, the subway seems to have exerted some influence prior to its opening. But it must be remembered that this region is different from those already reviewed. Here land values have been rising rapidly, space is at a premium, and anything which will enhance accessibility to such space will probably stimulate the rate of increase in land value. It appears that a subway reflects the conditions of the sections through which it passes, in any influences which it might exert upon land values. If the district is growing rapidly, the subway usually accelerates such growth; where it is stagnant, the values along the subway route change little; where influences are such as to cause land values to drop, the subway fails to pull the area in question from the slump which it is experiencing. It also seems to be true from the experience of this locality, that real estate operators may suddenly call into existence, new land values in sections which have possessed transit facilities before, but where no appreciable gains in land values had been experienced. A development, stimulating demand for a certain locality, has the effect of increasing land values. This may take place during the constructon of a new subway, directly after it is opened, or many years after it has served the area, or it may even occur in a territory not supplied with transit facilities at all, but otherwise accessible from regions so supplied. In other words, the subway may help to make possible a growth in land values. It does not cause the increase.

CHAPTER VI

THE CENTRAL PARK AREA

THE influence of the New York Central improvement in the area surrounding Park Avenue became even more noticeable in the East Central Park area north of 59th to 96th Street. From the environment which has already been described for the Park Avenue district before the improvement was made, this section developed into an elite residential district with high-class apartments and the finest residences. From Fifth to Park Avenue, this movement has spread, and much of the growth has been at the expense of Riverside Drive, which has lost some of its leading families in this shuffle.

At 96th Street, the northward drive of this development came to an abrupt halt, very noticeable in land values. This was due to the emergence of the New York Central lines on an elevated system north of that street and also, perhaps, to the existence of a somewhat mixed population in this quarter. Still further north, is the Harlem section, or black belt, where almost the whole population is colored.

Along Lexington Avenue runs the subway—the only subway in this area, since 1918. Before that time, the Second and Third Avenue elevated lines were the only transit systems. This avenue has taken on more of a commercial character than the avenues west of it. The Fifth Avenue buses and the private cars and taxicabs are a favorite means of conveyance for a large number of the users of the residential property adjoining Central Park, but to the users of Lexington Avenue properties, which now house many commercial structures, the subway is an essential. Despite the existence of the elevated lines within this area, it may said that the subway contributed greatly to the accessbility of the uptown East Side in providing five new stations for this area.

Prior to 1913, land values between Central Park and Third Avenue increased very slowly. Between 1905 and 1913, an increase of only 10 per cent was evident. With the completion of the New York Central improvement in 1913, and the opening of the subway five years later, land values increased on an average of 80 per cent below 80th Street, to over 100 per cent above that Street, but individual gains along the avenues ran higher than 300 per cent. Like in most other parts of Manhattan, however, the war years retarded this development—the greater part of these increases coming in the years since 1921.

The transformation of the land north of 80th Street and east of Third Avenue, from vacant parcels and cheap tenements to a developed section, later housing large apartments, accounts for the rise there. In 1913, the land was worth 35 per cent more than it was in 1905. By 1929 it gained an additional 93 per cent. The land experiencing the greater part of this growth was east of Second Avenue for from 1905 to 1913, the land between Second and Third Avenues gained by only 18 per cent while east of Second Avenue, land values rose by more than 45 per cent. Since 1913, the gain in the former strip was 70 per cent, whereas the latter rose by more than 100 per cent and by several hundred per cent in individual cases.

The land between this section around Carl Schurz Park, and the Sutton Place development further south, also rose by some 70 per cent between 1913 and 1929. The recent venture of Vincent Astor into this section, and the announcement of the Chapin and Brearly Schools in the Carl Schurz Park district, have furthered this "Far East" growth.

Avenue A has been renamed York Avenue, and cold water flats have been replaced by elegant apartments.

A great future development is contemplated in tnis region. There has been active buying of large areas in this vicinity just south of Carl Schurz Park—especially between York Avenue and East End Avenue. At present there are mainly four and six-story tenement houses here, but they are being hemmed in on all sides by some of the finest apartment houses in Manhattan. One of the foremost apartment experts in the city has envisioned York Avenue as a second Park Avenue within the next few years. Already there are plans on foot to build a huge apartment city here, overlooking the East River, and to cater to the most exclusive residents of the city, duplicating the work of Fred French further south, in even grander style. It has been suggested that a fleet of swift motor ferries might be operated to the foot of the financial center, connecting the offices downtown with the uptown river-front apartment homes, eliminating the use of crowded trains, and assuring the exclusiveness desired. The contemplated automobile drive on the eastern fringe of the island, would probably help to make complete the transformation of the East Side into a residential section of the well-to-do. With two elevated lines which have stood for many decades intervening between this section and the new subway, the rise of this new development can scarcely be attributed to changes in transit facilities. Yet, outside of the heart of the midtown section in Manhattan, this area has witnessed one of the most sensational changes in land value within recent years.

On the West Side of Central Park, there arises a new situation. This territory was served up to 96th Street by one elevated line, and one subway in 1905. Since that time no changes have been made in transit facilities. The land east of Ninth Avenue, or that which lies in the so-called central core is here a strip of only one block in width, between Ninth Avenue and Central Park. It is served by the Ninth Avenue elevated line. In its southern portion, the Broadway subway of the I. R. T. crosses it, and it is served by one station there. The rest of the subway line is two blocks west of Ninth Avenue. From 1905-1913, the land south of 80th Street gained by 32 per cent while that north of that street gained by 12 per cent. Since 1913, the land values have risen by over 100 per cent in the former region, and just under 100 per cent in the latter. In the meantime, the Eighth Avenue subway (equipped with five stations) is being constructed along Central Park West. From the Fall of 1922, to 1924, land values along Central Park West gained less than six per cent. From 1924 to 1926 an increase of 43 per cent was shown, and from 1926 to 1928, another gain of 20 per cent making a total advance in values since 1924 of 72 per cent. Here is a section which is getting its first subway. It is already well built up with apartments and hotels facing Central Park. The desirability of the Park location has already been a factor in stimulating these developments. The subway will no doubt make possible a more profitable use of much of this property. There is good reason to believe that much of this rise has been induced by speculation over the future growth of this avenue. At points where the stations are to be opened, the concentration in values is especially marked. Of course, it must not be overlooked that the selection of the already popular streets of 59th, 72nd, 79th, 86th, and 96th accounts for part of this concentration in values.

It should, however, be noticed that a somewhat similar change is occurring in the adjoining area which has been equipped with a subway since 1904. Land values here rose somewhat faster than the more easterly section between 1905 and 1913, increasing by 44 per cent on the average. Since

1913, the land has shown an average gain in value of slightly less than 100 per cent, the greater part of which has come in the last few years. The gradual rise of the City further northward in its demands for space, caused this vicinity to grow in value. The transportation was already provided; demand was all that was necessary. With the shortage of housing after the War, the apartments of these districts were gladly sought. The exclusive Riverside Drive, was responsible for some of the value increases in the extreme West of this section. Reference has already been made to the tendency for the residential development to move off the "backbone" of the island, and over to the river fronts.

Summarizing the experiences through which land values passed in the Central Park area of the City, it can be said that since 1913, they practically doubled throughout the entire section; that the greater part of this change came in the post-war years, when there was a heavy expansion movement of the City into this area, and that the largest percentage gains were recorded along the river sections rather than in the central core. It is difficult to prove that land adjoining transit lines through this district has enjoyed any more prosperity than land not so situated.

CHAPTER VII

North of 96th Street

North of 96th Street, to 118th Street on the East Side, the section can be analyzed rather closely. From Fifth Avenue to Park Avenue, there are no transit facilities. The strip from Park Avenue to Third Avenue has the Lexington Avenue subway running through its center. From Third Avenue to the East River, the only transit facilities are two elevated lines. From the year 1905 to 1913, the first of these strips gained by 24 per cent; the second and the third each gained approximately 45 per cent in land values. Since that time, the first strip has gained 42 per cent more, the second 23 per cent, and the third 15 per cent. The transit line undoubtedly helped to hasten the growth of this area. The character of the neighborhood, as has been mentioned before, militated against the continued rise which had begun in the real estate boom prior to 1911.

Much the same thing is found north of 118th Street up to the Harlem River, and for the same reasons. Between Lenox and Park Avenues and between Park Avenue and the River, land values gained almost 30 per cent in the years 1905-1913. Since 1913, the latter section gained 20 per cent while the former area advanced only five per cent. Both strips lie in the Black Belt, or negro settlement of New York.

On the West Side, between Columbus and Morningside Avenues and the Hudson River, the transit situation is very much the same as was seen further south. The subway and one elevated line have been the sole transit facilities since 1905. From 1905-1913, values rose 60 per cent. Since

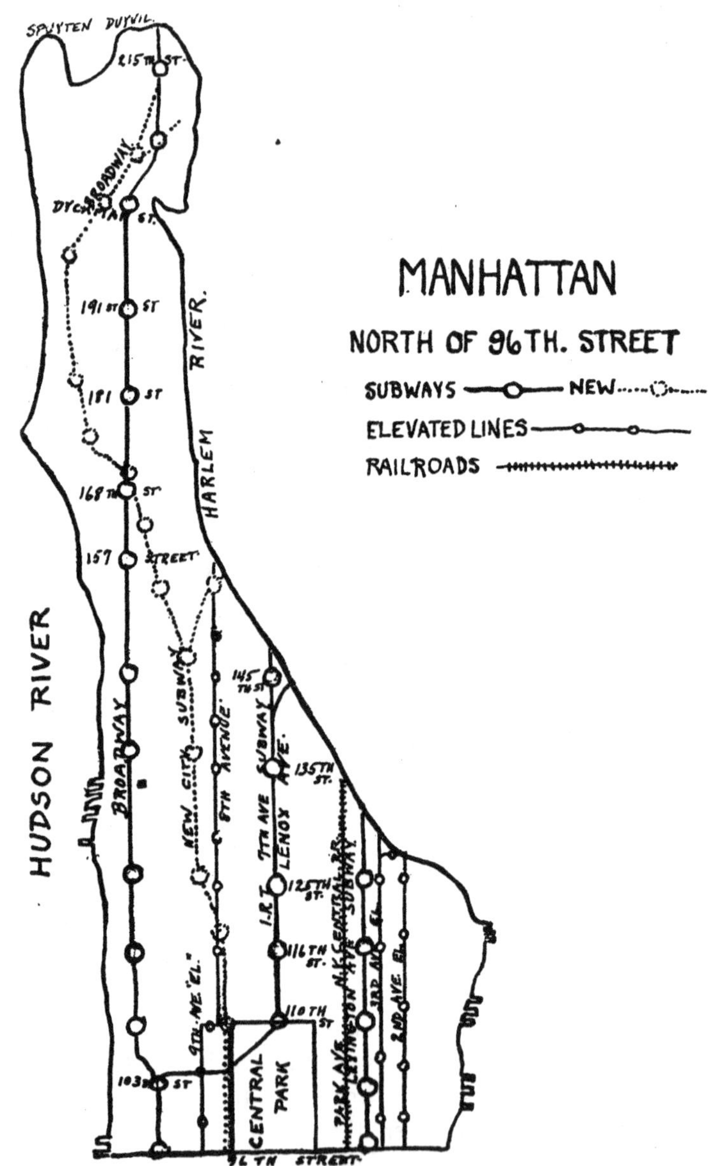
MANHATTAN
NORTH OF 96TH. STREET
SUBWAYS NEW
ELEVATED LINES
RAILROADS
SPUYTEN DUYVIL
215TH ST.
BROADWAY
DYCKMAN ST.
191 ST ST
181 ST
168TH ST
157 STREET
HARLEM RIVER
HUDSON RIVER
BROADWAY
NEW CITY SUBWAY
8TH AVENUE
145 TH ST
135TH ST.
7TH AVE
LENOX AVE.
SUBWAY
I.R.T.
125TH ST.
116TH ST.
110TH ST
9TH AVE "EL."
N.Y. CENTRAL R.R.
LEXINGTON AVE SUBWAY
PARK AVE.
3RD AVE EL
2ND AVE. EL
CENTRAL PARK
103RD ST
96TH STREET

1913, they have made a similar gain of 60 per cent. This corresponds to a like movement in land values, which was found to be taking place further downtown, along the western waterfront property in the Riverside Drive area. From Columbus Avenue to Lenox Avenue, the elevated road, and an arm of the subway served the area. Here however, increases of but 39 per cent for the first period, and 30 per cent for the second period were noted. Three stations of the new subway will be accessible in this latter section. Although the section as a whole showed a smaller increase in value since 1913, than before that year, some of the land adjoining Central Park along the route of the new subway has shown a rapid increase in the last few years. Since 1924, land values here have doubled. North of Central Park, however, along the subway route, the value of the land has not moved any more rapidly than the rate of growth throughout the section.

This is clearly shown in the territory lying between Morningside and Convent Avenues and Lenox Avenue, from 116th Street to the Harlem River, which was also served by these same transit facilities since 1905. Up to 1913, a gain of 29 per cent was made south of 137th Street and of 60 per cent north of that street. The lower portion gained but slightly since, while the upper portion actually showed a loss. The northeastern part of this strip is part of the Harlem colored district, and values have either remained at a standstill here, or have actually dropped. No very striking changes in land value have occurred in this section, along the new subway route.

There now remains the northern end of Manhattan. This presents an interesting case, since it was without transit facilities until 1904, when the first subway was built. No new transit has been extended here since, except the new subway, now under construction. The increases in land value in this part of the island have been very large, the greatest increases coming before 1913. The gains have varied in proportion to the distance of the land from the center of the City—the more northerly sections gaining the most. From 138th to 155th Streets, east of Convent Avenue, the gain from 1905-1929 was 136 per cent and from 155th Street to Spuyten Duyvil, 245 per cent. For these same areas, the increases fom 1905 to 1913 were 100 per cent and 130 per cent, respectively.

This is the same district which the City Club studied in 1910. This is the area which it cited in showing the great increases in value to which the subway gave rise. The reason for choosing this area, it was said, was to get away from the miscellaneous things which would interfere with a clear discernment of the unadulterated effects of transit extension. The following is an extract from the report of the City Club. It is often quoted[1]:

> The aggregate rise in this land from 135th Street to Spuyten Duyvil was about $69,300,000. If an estimated normal rise of $20,100,000 based upon the rise of the previous seven years be subtracted from this, it leaves a rise of about $49,200,000, apparently due to the building of the subway, which is 104 per cent increase on the value of 1900. . . . The cost of the entire subway from the Battery to the Sputen Duyvil and the West Farms Branch to Bronx Park was but $43,000,000. The property benefited in districts above noted could have paid this entire cost, and yet have a net profit, *due solely to its construction and operation.*

If this figure of $49,200,000 is to be taken as the value increase due solely to subway development between the years 1900-1908, it would, of course, follow that the landowners should pay for this increment in the value of their properties

[1] *Building of Rapid Transit Lines in New York City by Assessment upon Property Benefitted,* City Club of New York, October 2, 1908. Memo addressed to the Board of Estimate and Public Service Comm.

in the form of special assessments. Upon examination of the total value of this land, however, it would be found that this levy, if imposed, would amount to almost 50 per cent of the total. The arbitrary deduction of an allowance of $20,-100,000 for normal growth, based upon the rise of the previous seven years does not allow for a change in the rate of growth due to a conversion of land into other uses. In the "previous seven years" period, most of this land was still used for agricultural purposes, or else lay barren as vacant acreage. Most of the present streets were not yet cut through. After the opening of the Twentieth century, the land was gradually transformed into residential sites. A change of this kind will naturally be accompanied by rapid growth in value.

There is little doubt that an area never served by transit facilities before, will become tremendously more important for residential development when it is tapped by a rapid transit artery running through the heart of the City. But one point should not be overlooked. Although the subway may be the means of calling land into new uses, does *all* the increment in value arise from this cause? Consultation with leading development companies would lead one to believe otherwise. Estimates given out by some of the best known operators place the expected rise from converting raw land into land developed for residential use at from three to four times the original value. The work of gathering together a plot of land, surveying, grading, cutting into streets and lots, installing gas, water and other utilities, laying sidewalks and curbing, financing, and selling, requires this increase in value to make a development pay.

In a report of tht Regional plan of New York,[1] a similar estimate is made. For land which was subdivided and sold with

[1] *Land Values*, Lewis, Heydecker, O'Hara-Regional Plan of New York and Its Environs, 1927, p. 54.

parts of acreage allocated for streets but without local improvements, the estimated rise is 200 to 300 per cent of the base value, averaging 230 per cent. For land sold with all local improvements, the figures range from 250 to 800 per cent, averaging 415 per cent. Land potentially useful for high-class residences tends to show a higher gain ranging to about ten times the original raw value. The report further states that "land prices in partially built up areas . . . tend to approximate the values of fully built-up areas. This indicates that the prices asked by the developers and frequently obtained, approach the maximum value of the property when fully developed."

What was the condition of this land in the northern part of Manhattan when the subway was constructed? As has been mentioned, some of it was laid out into streets, some of it was built up, a great part of it, especially further north, was farm land. Three-quarters of the land was reported to be vacant. Residential growth was stimulated in the improved regions, and values rose there. When the land was in a raw state, subdividing was encouraged and great increases in land value followed this development. The fact that the more outlying sections showed a greater percentage increase over the original value than did areas similarly supplied with transit, but located nearer the center of the City tends to confirm the statement that a very large part of the growth in land values arose out of improvements incident to the subdividing. The conversion of farm land into land which is suitable for residential or business use, has the effect of multiplying its value many times. The subway appears to serve the purpose of increasing the possibilty of such conversion or of causing it to take place sooner than it would ordinarily require. To this extent it is instrumental in facilitating a rise in land values.

Mr. Lewis, in an entirely different connection, stresses the same idea that a multiplication of land values in property passing from the stage of acreage to city lots cannot be looked upon as indicative of the influence of any *one* particular factor which may have been present at the time the change occurred. Speaking of the effects of park areas upon adjoining properties, he says:[1]

As property changes from acreage to city lots the percentage of increase in value is greater than during any other period of development. Much of this advance in value may be speculative, but that there is a real increase due to the land having become marketable, cannot be questioned. During the period covered by the increase in taxable values about Central Park, the great northward movement in population and improvement began and there would undoubtedly have been a marked advance in value even if Central Park had not been bought and improved.

The rapid transformation of land which was used for farming not so long ago, into sites for large cooperative apartments today, explains some of the phenomenal increases in this neighborhood in recent years. The rise of Dyckman Street and 207th Streets as the main arteries of trade and retail activity in this region, has increased their values several hundred per cent over what they were in 1900.

It is interesting to note how recent some of this growth has been. The *New York Times* of Sunday, November 18th, 1928 writes on page 1 of Section 12:

The great feature in the Dyckman area during the last four years has been the rapidity of its development in the former small farm territory south of Dyckman Street. . . . With the exception of three or five walk-up flats on the Elwood Street frontage, that entire plot was practically vacant four years ago. Virtually every foot, however, was utilized for gardening. . . . The little farms have now disappeared. That block has been

[1] *Planning of the Modern City*, Nelson P. Lewis, p. 178.

bisected with the cutting through of Sickles Street from Sherman to Nagle Avenues, and on the two blocks, there are today more than twenty six-story apartment edifices, many of the elevator type, and several accommodating more than 100 families each.

The area referred to above was worth $745,000 in 1905. By 1913 it was worth $1,516,000. Streets were then cut through, taking away about one quarter of the land. The value of the remaining three quarters today is estimated at close to four million dollars.

The reason that all of this section has not shown an even greater rise in land values in recent years is that speculative buying in the earlier years discounted a great part of the expected future enhancement in values.

CHAPTER VIII

Borough of the Bronx

Like Manhattan, the Bronx may be said to have a central region in which there is a concentration of real estate activity, and in which is aggregated, the largest percentage of land values in the borough.

It will be convenient to divide this central core of the Bronx into two groups—an inner core, and an outer circle. (See Map).

The inner core is bounded by the East River and the Harlem River on the South, by Bronx Park on the North and by Southern Boulevard and Prospect Avenue on the East, with Webster and Morris Avenues on the West.

The outer circle spreads the eastern boundary to Woodycrest and University Avenues, the northern line to Woodlawn Cemetery and the western boundary to the Bronx River.

The entire central core consists of a section including about one-third of the land area of the Bronx, but constituting more than half of the total land value. The inner core is less than one-sixth of the area of the borough but forms about one-quarter of its land values.

The significant thing to consider with reference to this inner core is that it represented in 1905, the center of greatest activity in the borough. It possessed the two transit arteries: the Third Avenue elevated, and the Westchester Avenue line, which in 1904 ran as far as Bronx Park, as well as the Harlem Division of the New York Central R. R. In 1906, the Westchester Avenue line was connected by tunnel with the Lenox Avenue branch of the West side subway in Manhattan. Save for the Putnam Division of the New

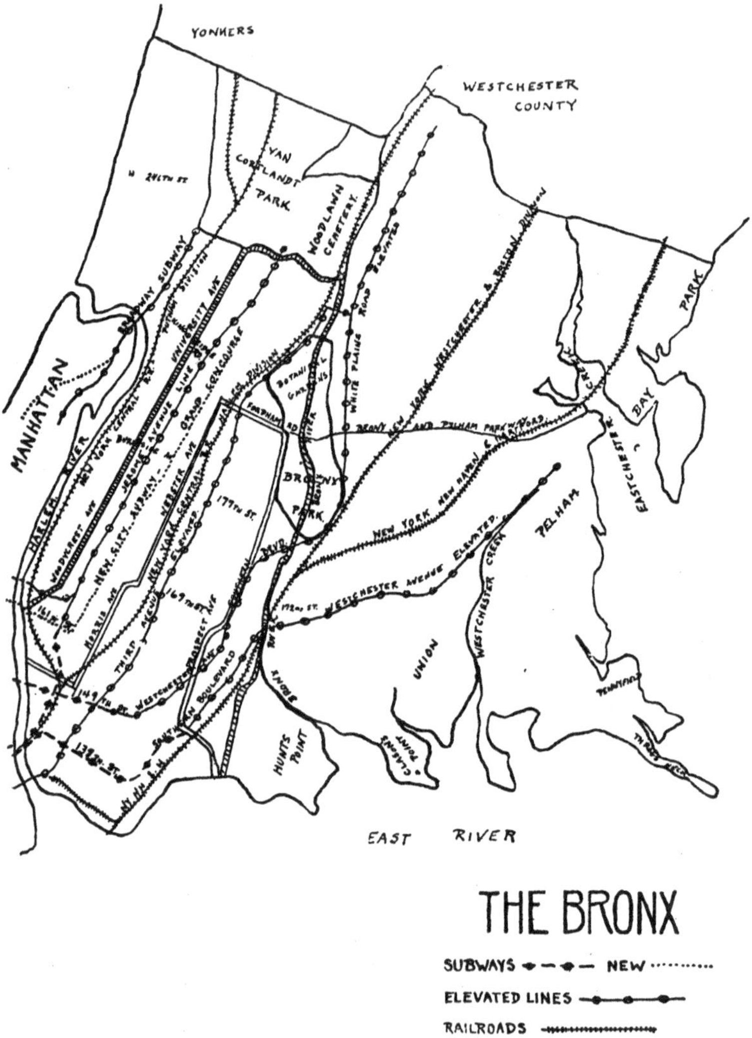

York Central R. R. along the Harlem River, and the New York New Haven & Hartford R. R. further over on the East

these were the only transportation routes serving the borough at the time.

The southern part of this inner core is proximate to Manhattan and was the first zone to be influenced by the extended growth of the island. The great majority of the factories, warehouses, loft buildings, office buildings, and larger stores were located in this district, although by far, the greater number of the buildings in the inner core were one family houses and tenements. In 1905, the value of this area was something more than 40 per cent of the land value of the entire borough.

When the area in the outer circle is studied along with the inner core, the significance of this central section becomes even more striking. In 1905, 70 per cent of all the dwellings —including both residences and tenements, were within its borders. Practically all of the loft buildings, warehouses and office buildings were located here (although they totaled less than 100 altogether); and about 85 per cent of all factories. This entire central region in 1905 had a land value of about two thirds of the borough value.

This is to be explained by the fact that the greater part of the Bronx was still very much undeveloped—a large percentage of it consisting of open fields and farms. In fact, approximately three-quarters of the land was vacant. Within the central zone itself, over one-third was still unimproved, especially in the outer circle.

Since that time, great changes have taken place. The population has increased from less than 275,000 to more than 950,000. Less than one-third of the land still remains vacant. The number of buildings has more than doubled and large apartments with many rooms have replaced the structures of smaller size. Vast improvements have been made in transit facilities.

The Third Avenue elevated road was the first rapid transit facility which connected the Bronx with Manhattan. In 1905, property along this transit route was worth considerably more than land in the adjoining territory, and from 1905 to 1913, this position continued to be held. Willis Avenue and Third Avenue and parts of Alexander Avenue were the business streets of this part of the borough, and as population increased, values continued to rise. The path of the elevated line along these streets was therefore marked by constantly increasing values between 1905 and 1913 along its entire route. Since 1913 this neighborhood has increased in value in some parts, other sections have remained at a standstill, and small declines have been evidenced in others. From 161st Street to 169th Street for example, 1929 land values are on the average from one to two per cent less than 1913 values. On the other hand, between 169th Street and Tremont Avenue, 1929 values have risen some 45 per cent above the values of 1913. During the war years, a slump was experienced, but since then, there has been a revival and values have been carried appreciably above their pre-war levels. Finally, between Tremont Avenue and Bronx Park on this line, gains have been slight—most of the property remaining at less than 10 per cent above the 1913 values, until 1927, when assessed valuations indicate a slight rise in value of a number of blocks. In the meantime, properties lying within a five-block radius on either side of the elevated route have passed through somewhat different value movements. In the southern tip of the Central Core, (the land lying nearest the East side of Manhattan) values only rose 15 per cent since the pre-war period. Between 161st Street and 169th Street, property has virtually remained at a standstill, east of the line, while it has increased 30 per cent west of it. Up to Tremont Avenue average gains have been 26 per cent, while north of that road, increases have been over 45 per cent.

This higher rate of growth indicated for the district around

Tremont Avenue and further north has occurred chiefly along Tremont Avenue and along 180th Street which are side streets perpendicular to Third Avenue, and which have enjoyed a retail trade coming from the passengers leaving the elevated stations at these streets. This increased business has been secured somewhat at the expense of Third Avenue.

What happened here was that land further south, and nearer the elevated line was developed at an earlier date than the remainng land. Inasmuch as this transit line was constructed before the opening of the Twentieth Century, 1905 values already reflected the advanced value of this property. Following 1905, a more rapid expansion of the borough began and the conversion of raw land into developed residential communities brought about rather large value increases. Although the inner core was the most built-up section of the borough at the opening of the century, there was still much improvement to be made. Both New York Central lines and the Third Avenue elevated system were there. It remained to develop communities which could take advantage of these facilities. Most of this expansion took place prior to 1913, the greatest gains being netted in those areas which were farthest north of Manhattan. This can be seen in referring to the same districts that were mentioned above, lying within a radius of five blocks on either side of the Third Avenue elevated. The southern tip gained 19 per cent from 1905 to 1913, the strip from 161st to 169th Street showed an average increase of 60 per cent, that from 169th to Tremont, 72 per cent, and that north of Tremont, to Bronx Park, 111 per cent.

Not much building activity has taken place along Third Avenue recently. In parts it is beginning to appear like sections along Third and Sixth Avenues in Manhattan, where it is felt that the elevated structure is keeping land values down. In any event, it does not appear that property fronting on this transit facility at present has any better chances for a value increase than any other property in the same neighborhood. On the contrary, the future may rather place such land at a disadvantage because of the tendency to regard the elevated structure as an objectionable encumbrance upon the abutting property. However, since this elevated road was already serving the borough in 1905, it would be more desirable to analyze changes which occurred along the paths of those lines which were more recently constructed.

The elevated system along Westchester Avenue and terminating at 180th Street was opened in 1904. It was connected with the Lenox Avenue branch of the Broadway subway of Manhattan in 1906. Along 149th Street, where the transit line enters the Bronx via subway, land values rose about 120 per cent between the date of its opening and 1913, and over 90 per cent more since that time—making a total of approximately 325 per cent between 1905 and 1929. This region, already highly developed, was undergoing further expansion. The subway no doubt helped to stimulate this movement. Most of this area was occupied by solid blocks of brick or frame houses of from one to five stories, with four and five story brick flats predominating. Along Third Avenue, Willis Avenue and Brook Avenue, which crossed this street, there were retail stores, and these also tended to spread along 149th, 150th and 151st Streets. Land values at these intersections naturally showed unusual gains. Especially was this marked where Third Avenue crosses 149th Street. Here was provided a transfer point, where elevated passengers had to change for the subway. Corner values at that point have multiplied manyfold and retail values have spread along Melrose Avenue, and Courtlandt Avenue, from here to 160th Street. This advantage has been somewhat limited in recent years, through the construction by the transit company of an under-cover passageway between subway and elevated lines. The retail zone mentioned, has, however, become well established.

Through Westchester Avenue and Southern Boulevard, retail stores are to be found along the greater part of the route; although in certain parts a miscellaneous collection of small buildings, auto shops, and garages are preponderant. Land values along these streets have moved into fairly high ground compared with their 1905 levels, although these increases have not been spread uniformly. At locations such as Jackson Avenue and Prospect Avenue gains of from 300 to 1000 per cent have been made since 1905. With bus and trolley line intersections at these points, coupled with their choice as sites for stations on the elevated line, it was natural for them to become centers of concentration and as a result, land values rose spectacularly. Both 163rd and 165th Streets had developed retail districts, and where they crossed Westchester Avenue and drew from the crowds coming from Simpson Street and Intervale Avenue stations, land values also tended to rise above the general level. This also holds for Tremont Avenue and 180th Street, both of which served with local surface car lines, made rapid strides in retail development, and were greatly benefited by the increasing annual passenger traffic which issued from the stations of the I. R. T. onto these streets. The properties lying between these stations along the elevated road and that at a distance of two or three blocks away from the route have also shown increases, although not as great. They show on the average, a present doubling of 1905 land values. Through this district there is a scattering of one and two story residences, and considerable numbers of four to six story brick flats, a number of garages, repair shops, auto supply stores, car yards, and vacant land.

The White Plains line, running north above East 180th Street to East 241st Street, was made part of the contract arrangements of 1913 and formed an extension to the elevated road just referred to. It was opened for operation in 1917.

This route extends outside of the central zone of the Bronx and serves an area, long without rapid transit facilities. During the first decade of the century, a gradual rise in the land values here was perceptible, but almost all of it was undeveloped for urban purposes and not until 1913 did the City break it up into lots on the city tax maps. Up to that time it had been referred to as values per acre of farm land. Since 1913, the land immediately fronting along White Plains Road and along the cross streets that lead away from stations has shown gains of about three to ten times the value of that year, and other properties within a half mile range of the stations have multiplied by from two to five times. Since the war, hundreds of one and two family houses have been erected, and this entire area is becoming a large residential community for a New York working population, commuting on a five cent fare. Further towards the East in the direction of Pelham Bay the land is still vacant for the greater part, and as a matter of fact, little developed in any respects. Land values here have changed little since 1913. There is no direct transit facility to Manhattan through here, and for that reason it has been less desirable for residential purposes than the more westerly areas through which the elevated line passes. Here, then, is a good illustration of an area which has most of the qualities for desirable real estate development, save accessibility. Where this situation exists, and such accessibility is provided, the result seems to be to move land values upward in excess of what it would cost to convert raw land into improved lots. This is especially true along those streets which are potentially useful for retail purposes in such areas.

The extension of the Lexington Avenue subway into the

Bronx, via 138th Street and then into Southern Boulevard and across the Bronx River as an elevated structure along Westchester Avenue was completed in 1918. Work began on the construction about 1913. In following the course of land values along this subway some very interesting comparisons come up for attention.

The first stretch of subway is along East 138th Street where four stations are located. Here the value of the area within a two-block range for selected blocks on each side of the subway was $3,769,000 in 1905. In 1913, it was $5,-753,000. The subway was definitely planned in that year. In 1917—a year before the line was opened, the land was worth $5,774,000. In 1921, three years after the subway was opened, the land value in this same district was $5,744,000 and in 1929 it had become $6,885,000, or a trifle less than 20 per cent over 1913 values.

The district served by this line was already well built up by 1913. From 1905-1913 the process of development still continued and land values rose. By 1913, however, the character of the neighborhood had been stamped rather clearly. It consisted mostly of factories, warehouses, lumber yards and freight terminals near the rivers, and immediately fronting on the subway route, four, five and six story brick tenements with a scattering of one and two family houses. As can be seen from the figures given, a subway through this region did very little to disturb existing values. The increase since 1921 is a reflection of the tendency for land values throughout the City to rise somewhat above pre-war levels, due to the new purchasing power of the dollar, and can hardly be regarded as arising out of any material advance in the intrinsic merit of the property.

If the path of the subway is followed closely to a section just a bit further north, however, a somewhat different condition will be noted; near the foot of 138th Street the subway turns into Southern Boulevard, where there are four stations up to 163rd Street. Along the first part of this stretch, it passes through much the same kind of neighborhood as that just described, and the behavior of land values is similar, though slightly better. Values just about doubled between 1905 and 1913, and since the time of the opening of the subway, made another gain of over 25 per cent. Sites along Southern Boulevard, valuable for retail purposes, and some of the residential blocks around St. Mary's Park, and near the 143rd Street station tended to rise, but for the most part, this section offered little inducement for anything other than industrial purposes. The main improvements along the subway route through here have been garages and four and six story flats.

The large freight terminal of the New York, New Haven & Hartford Railroad makes this region especially desirable for industrial uses, and these were already well established when the subway was built through here.

North of Leggett Avenue to 163rd Street, the subway leaves the inner core and enters the outer circle. Here the territory was less built up than the southerly section along the subway route, and hence provided more opportunities for expansion. Southern Boulevard has come in for a retail development in parts along here, especially at 163rd Street which has become an important retail street, and which is provided with a subway station at Southern Boulevard. At this corner land values stood at seven times above the 1905 figures in 1913, and in 1929, they were twelve times the 1905 values. This has become a great concentration point and has drawn surrounding retail values to itself. For blocks selected along this part of the subway route, it has been found that from 1905 to 1913 there was an average tripling of land values, and that these have gained from 50 to 80 per cent since, making 1929 values about six times as great as those noted for 1905. North of 163rd Street and crossing the Bronx River, the transit route continues as an elevated line. No material difference between land values along the subway routes as compared with the elevated line is observable in this region other than the fact that values multiplied to a greater extent along the latter than along the former route.

This does not indicate that an elevated line is more serviceable in calling higher land values into being than is a subway. It simply reflects the fact that as the route is followed further north, it spreads a greater and greater distance away from the central core, and out into the periphery, which, like the Pelham Bay district previously described, was in 1905 still evaluated in terms of acres of farm land, whereas today it has become developed into city lots. Many of these are improved with modern residences, stores and apartments. The result is that great gains have been recorded along this part of the transit route. The stimulus which it might be said the line gave to this section, however, did not manifest itself immediately. The most spectacular increases in value came when the building activity after the war spread into those areas available for residential construction. Since 1921, a rise of five times over the values in that year has been common. In fact, over a broad area—covering one-half mile on each side of Westchester Avenue, an average gain of over 150 per cent has been made since 1921. This includes many vacant lots which are still potential sites for desirable residential improvements.

This increase in value which arises in a section when raw land is converted into developed lots is also seen in a neighboring area, which has not received any rapid transit facilities except the two trolley lines which it already had. In 1905, Hunts Point was little developed. Since that time there has been some improvement. Although there is still a good deal of vacant land there, there have been erected many more shops, factories, garages, and two and four story brick houses. Population has, of course, increased. The value of this whole section in 1905 was placed at $2,931,000. By 1929 it was worth $14,148,000.

The Jerome Avenue line opened a wide territory to additional rapid transit facilities in 1917. Parts of this area had already been served by the New York Central R. R. but rapid transportation into downtown Manhattan on a five cent fare was a new convenience. The district had already been growing rapidly, especially in the southern part of the outer circle.

In the pre-war period, the land within the outer circle served by this transit line made a gain of about 60 per cent south of 169th Street, and almost trebled in value further to the north. This, was, of course, before the elevated line was built, but real estate was nevertheless being developed. Both the Putnam and the Harlem divisions of the New York Central then served this area.

This early real estate activity practically ceased during the war years, and in 1921 values were not very much more than they had been in 1913. But since 1921, land values along the entire region served by the Jerome Avenue line have again trebled in value. Did the transit line cause this rise?

This is a difficult question. It must be remembered that the Grand Boulevard and Concourse parallels this elevated line along its entire course, and that in the years 1921-1929 there has been a great deal of elevator apartment construction in the adjoining territory. On Walton Avenue, facing the 162nd Street entrance to the Concourse, a large six story fireproof apartment was erected. Then, between 164th and 172nd Streets, all along Gerard, Walton, Sherman and Grant Avenues, and along the Concourse, large new apartment houses have been constructed. Along Jerome Avenue in this vicinity, there are many vacant lots, with a sprinkling of garages and auto shops and salesrooms here and there, and a miscellaneous assortment of buildings. From 170th Street, north, Jerome Avenue assumes somewhat more of a retail character, especially around stations. At Burnside Avenue, the New York University students pass to and from trains in great numbers daily. This has made the street a valuable retail zone. The rest of Jerome Avenue, however, is built up with from one to five story houses, and garages, and larger stretches are still vacant. North of 172nd Street, some of the valuable property along the Grand Concourse is occupied by large automobile salesrooms and by a number of new apartments such as the thirteen-story elevator apartment at Clifford Place. Above Kingsbridge Road most of the land assumes a more uniformly built up character of small homes with a few flats and tenements and with an occasional crosstown street of retail character, usually on the site of an elevated station. Along Grand Concourse from Kingsbridge Road to 199th Street, some fairly large apartments have been constructed.

Yet, when land values along individual blocks throughout this section are examined, it will be discovered that there has been a fairly even distribution in the growth already cited, despite this somewhat mottled external appearance in the realty developments, except for the fact that Jerome Avenue seems to have enjoyed fewer of the advantages which the elevated line might have given to the rest of the district. It appears that a cheap accessible line to Manhattan was desirable, but that the retail district which might normally be expected to develop along the route of the line has, so far at least failed to materialize satisfactorily. The side streets have gained mostly in this direction. This has already been observed to have occurred in a similar way along the Third Avenue line. Furthermore, ready access to the large department stores in midtown Manhattan has stunted any growth of material size in the retail business. In view of the somewhat rapid rise in values throughout this entire district, without the same more or less homogeneous external evidences to be found in realty developments, however, this district has been less satisfactory for treatment in the present analysis. There has evidently been a fair amount of discounting of anticipated future growth here.

Taking the experiences which have been found for the entire borough of the Bronx, however, the following seems to hold true:

(1) Centers of concentration have their values greatly enhanced by transit lines which augment this centralizing effect.

(2) Transit lines do little to stimulate land values in an otherwise " dead " area.

(3). In districts which have been well established with certain definite characteristics, there will probably be less influence by new transit facilities than in less developed areas.

(4) In areas not supplied with transit, the effect of extending such transit will be noticeable in a rise in land values, provided such a district is ready for development.

(5) A zone supplied with a railroad running into the heart of the city, on a monthly commutation fare, will probably evidence additional growth if a five-cent transit line is extended into it.

(6) It is not true that the land immediately abutting upon a rapid transit line always derives the greatest benefit from it.

(7) Elevated structures may later exert a depressing effect upon properties along which they are built even

though the reverse effect seems to be evidenced at the start.

(8) The influences of transit lines upon property values can be explained only in terms of all other environmental conditions of the area through which they pass.

CHAPTER IX

Borough of Brooklyn

Each borough seems to have its small center of concentration, in which are grouped the daily business activities of a large part of its population, and in which the values of the land reflect this demand for space within the boundaries of a limited area. In Brooklyn, this is the Borough Hall district—which, in size, compares with the downtown business zone of Manhattan, being a trifle over two per cent of the area of this large borough, but amounting to considerably more than ten per cent of the land value of Brooklyn. In 1905, this small area formed 15 per cent of the total land values. The opening of outlying regions in the borough, however, has somewhat reduced this relative importance in recent years.

It is in this part of Brooklyn that are congregated the large office buildings which are beginning to make a rival skyline to that of Manhattan, directly across the river; the borough's most important hotels, the Municipal government buildings, the main offices of banks, brokerage houses, real estate and insurance companies and trust companies; the large department stores—in a word—it is the business heart of the borough. It is more than this. In its eastern end, in the vicinity of Flatbush Avenue, it has been developing a theater zone which shows signs of becoming a Times Square of Brooklyn.

Twenty transit stops are located here and five more will be provided by the new subway. All subway lines were built after the beginning of the century. Twelve of these stations are on elevated lines, all of which existed in 1900.

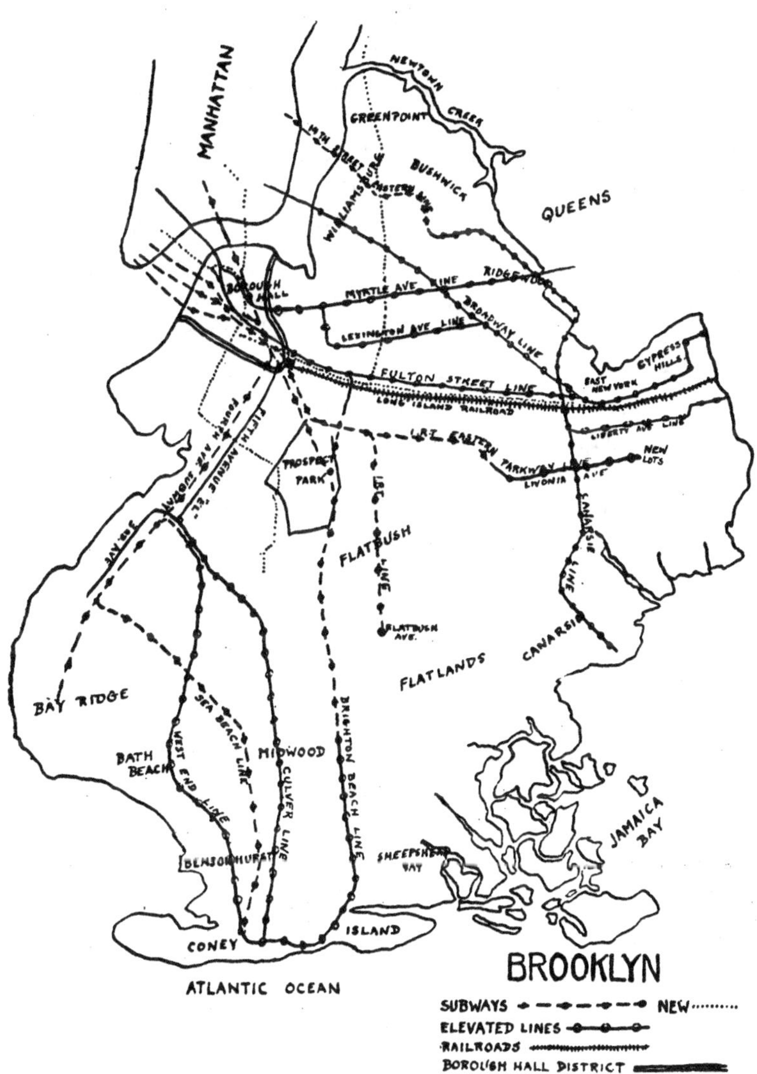
MANHATTAN
NEWTOWN CREEK
GREENPOINT
BUSHWICK
QUEENS
WILLIAMSBURG
BOROUGH HALL
MYRTLE AVE LINE
RIDGEWOOD
BROADWAY LINE
LEXINGTON AVE LINE
FULTON STREET LINE
LONG ISLAND RAILROAD
EAST NEW YORK
CYPRESS HILLS
LIBERTY AVE LINE
EASTERN PARKWAY
NEW LOTS
LIVONIA AVE
PROSPECT PARK
FIFTH AVENUE EL.
FOURTH AVE SUBWAY
FLATBUSH
FLATBUSH AVE.
CANARSIE LINE
CANARSIE
FLATLANDS
BAY RIDGE
BATH BEACH
SEA BEACH LINE
WEST END LINE
MIDWOOD
CULVER LINE
BRIGHTON BEACH LINE
BENSONHURST
SHEEPSHEAD BAY
JAMAICA BAY
CONEY ISLAND
ATLANTIC OCEAN
BROOKLYN
SUBWAYS
NEW
ELEVATED LINES
RAILROADS
BOROUGH HALL DISTRICT

The Brooklyn extension of the Lexington Avenue line in Manhattan was completed and put into operation to Borough Hall, and then to Atlantic and Flatbush Avenues in 1908. Contracts for this work were made as early as 1902. Work was started on the Fourth Avenue line in 1907, although it was not put into operation through the Borough Hall district and connected with Manhattan by the Montague Street tunnel, until 1920. The new I. R. T. tunnel coming into Brooklyn at Clark Street was opened in 1919. By 1920 then, this region had obtained all of its present transit facilities. Between 1905 and 1920 it showed a slow steady rise of about 45 per cent. Since that time it has grown more rapidly and land values have risen by slightly less than 100 per cent. It was during this post-war development that Brooklyn completed its new Municipal Building, its new Chamber of Commerce building and a dozen other large office buildings. The department stores expanded and modernized their headquarters. New hotels and elevator-apartments were constructed, and the St. George Hotel was remodeled so that it is now the largest in the city. Several very large theaters were also erected, notably, the Paramount and the Fox, on Flatbush Avenue. This movement has not stopped. It is proceeding more rapidly than ever. Along the route of the new city subway through this region many old buildings have been demolished so as to facilitate the cutting through of the subway. Modern and larger buildings are taking the place of these older structures. Year after year the old two and four-story frame or brick houses which have stood for generations are being replaced with up-to-date lofts and office buildings.

Although land values in this district have on the average trebled since 1905, the gains in some parts have been much greater—ranging as high as five and six hundred per cent on certain blocks along Court, Fulton, Bridge and Willoughby Streets and Flatbush Avenue. These increases are especially significant in view of the fact that this was already a highly developed zone with values running as high in 1905 along Fulton Street as $5,000 per front foot. The concentration movement which gained headway here since the war shows indications of continuing for some time, and any increase in transit facilities through here will probably help to augment this development. Like the midtown and downtown sections of Manhattan, this area has become a focal point. Like them, it has drawn its own strength away from others, for the business of its department stores has undoubtedly been increased at the expense of the big stores on Broadway, and its theaters have prospered from patronage that would otherwise have gone to smaller local amusement houses, or to theaters in Manhattan. Unlike them, it is less fortunately situated geographically, as a natural converging point, for the borough is so large and its population so spread out that no natural conversion point seems to exist. However, the construction of all rapid transit (including the new subway line) in Brooklyn, has been made so as to converge into the Borough Hall section before crossing over to Manhattan, so that this has become the " neck of the bottle " so to speak, for Manhattan-bound passenger traffic. With stations provided in this zone on all lines coverging here, it has become so easily accessible as to make it a greater center of activity. Only a new system of transit routing could detract from its importance in this respect.

East of this downtown business section lies a large district between Flushing Avenue and Atlantic Avenue and between Bedford Avenue and Broadway. Through this region run the Myrtle Avenue elevated line, the Lexington Avenue line and the Fulton Street elevated, and on its eastern border is the Broadway line, while on its south is the Long Island Railroad. All of these transit systems served this area before 1900. In addition to these, a network of trolley lines is spread through here. Residential development was begun somewhat early, and in 1905 less than five per cent of this land was still vacant. In 1905, the value of the land was approximately fifty million dollars. In 1913 it was seventy million. Today it is placed at close to ninety million. This represents a growth considerably below the average for the borough. These figures include the important retail properties along Fulton Street, Nostrand Avenue and Broadway, but on Broadway itself, which at one time was considered to be the most important retail business street in Brooklyn, values have not kept pace with the rate of growth evidenced by other retail streets in the borough. Like the Borough Hall district, this region had an early start. Unlike it, it has not become a great concentration center. It has remained primarily a residential zone, with flats and tenement houses a prevailing class. Of this latter type of building, this section has more than half of all those in the entire borough. Moreover, a more or less mixed population like that in northeastern Manhattan lives here. At present it offers little opportunity for new development. The new subway will pass along both the western and southern portions of this section. It may stimulate growth along the retail streets here. There is little likelihood that it will provoke any marked changes in the rest of the territory. It is not transit that it needs.

The Greenpoint, Bushwick, Williamsburgh and Ridgewood sections of Brooklyn have made very little progress in real estate expansion since the turn of the century. Whereas the average increase in land values for the entire borough has been over 300 per cent in the last quarter century, this section has advanced but 80 per cent during the same period. Moreover, the greatest advance in values in Brooklyn has taken place since the war, but for this region the land values have risen little more than 20 per cent since that time.

Throughout this district, especially along the waterfronts of Greenpoint and of Williamsburgh, and along a freight spur of the Long Island Railroad, there are a considerable number of industrial properties—about half of all the factories in Brooklyn being located here. The greater part of this area, however, is improved with residential structures—some 30,000 buildings out of 36,000, being of this type with more than half of these consisting of four-story flats and tenements. Before 1913, the Broadway elevated line ran as far as the East River to the Broadway Ferry and the Myrtle Avenue line some distance away, made connection to Manhattan via the Brooklyn Bridge. A system of trolley lines made this district accessible to these transit routes. No direct connection to Manhattan was provided for this region, however, until the Broadway line was connected to Manhattan via the Williamsburgh Bridge and Center Street loop under the 1913 contracts, and until the 14th Street Eastern line was built through the heart of this area. The former was opened in 1913. The latter was put into operation as far as Bushwick Avenue in 1924, but the elevated extension of this subway to Eastern Parkway and Broadway was not completed until 1928.

Following the course of land values along the 14th Street-Eastern line, it is immediately seen that any hopes for an extraordinarily large increase in land values as a result of the construction of the subway have so far at least, been doomed to disappointment. Taking the land one block deep on each side of this route, it is found that along the subway up to Bushwick Avenue, which was opened in 1924, land values declined between 1913 and 1924 by a slight amount. Between the date of the opening, and the present, land on the streets directly adjoining the stations gained as much as 50 per cent on the average, but along the rest of the route showed less than a 20 per cent increase over the 1913 level.

Along the elevated extension from Bushwick Avenue to Broadway and Eastern Parkway, the behavior of land values was somewhat more satisfactory, especially further East in the direction of Ridgewood—showing an average gain between 1913 and 1929 of better than 60 per cent and at some stations, an increase of as much as 100 per cent. These increases are along the borough boundary line between Brooklyn and Queens and represent a somewhat different territory than the rest of the district referred to, since they are on the fringe of a new section which has been opened more recently for residential development.

The changes in property values along the route of this new line are an excellent illustration of the environmental influences upon the effects which such a facility might be deemed to produce. Most of this area has remained static since the war. The buildings are old and there is a little vacant land available for new construction. Along some of the side streets leading to transit stations there have been some changes in the improvement of retail sites. In the residential part of the district, however, most of those desiring to better their living quarters have moved to more remote parts of Brooklyn or Queens. Needless to say this migration of the more progressive class of its tenants has not materially aided realty values here.

The extension of the Interborough lines from the Atlantic Avenue terminal to Utica Avenue along Eastern Parkway parallels the 14th Street Eastern line, but is some three miles further south. Although this vicinity already had access to the Long Island Railroad and to the Fulton Street elevated line, this was the first rapid direct route, to all points on Manhattan Island. It was opened in 1920. Since that year, average land values have more than doubled between Prospect Park and Buffalo Avenue; Eastern Parkway, St. John's Place and Montgomery Street, paralleling the subway, as well as Utica, Schnectady, Troy and Albany Avenues have made unusually large gains. On the basis of 1913 values, the land values along these streets have risen from two to eight times. This takes in a fairly large area. In 1913, 15 per cent of the land was unimproved. Less than five per cent is now vacant. Utica and Nostrand Avenues have increased their retail frontage and part of St. John's Place is also given over to retail space. The rest of this region has gone through a remarkable transformation in some parts. A great number of new private residences have been erected, but what is more important, there has been much construction of modern apartment houses along Eastern Parkway, and along sidestreets and on avenues immediately adjoining.

The elevated extension of this subway to New Lots in 1922 also started building activity there. In 1921, 15 per cent of this land was still vacant. Here also, less than five per cent now remains unimproved. Gains through this region as a whole have been fairly great, but immediately adjacent to the elevated route they have been more moderate. The most important gains in land value have been experienced along Sutter and Pitkin Avenues — two big retail streets, paralleling the new elevated line. Pitkin Avenue, west of Snedeker Avenue has an elevated line of its own, which has been standing for years. Rockaway Avenue, a side street, perpendicular to the avenues mentioned, has also gone through a more rapid development than the rest of the area. The property along the streets referred to, is the most valuable land in this district. It has, no doubt, been stimulated greatly through the increased buying population which additional transit facilities have brought to this area; for land values along Sutter Avenue and Pitkin Avenue have risen several hundred per cent since 1913, and a large part of this increase has come since 1921. Along Livonia Avenue, however, where the elevated line is constructed, average values have slightly less than doubled for the period 1913-1929. This is no better than the average gain for the whole district. Here is a case where the transit line was not, as is generally the case, erected along the existing center of concentration of the district and hence did little more than to enhance the value of an established zone three blocks away, rather than to participate in it. Thus far, commercial development along Livonia Avenue has been slow. In fact, in addition to the retail streets mentioned, Belmont and Blake Avenues, and parts of a great number of side streets in this region have seemed to show more promise of retail growth than does Livonia Avenue. Most of the streets through here are zoned for business purposes. Whether Livonia Avenue can succeed in drawing away the Sutter Avenue trade is at present very doubtful. However, it is too early to judge the final results. For the present, any stimulus which it might be said the I. R. T. line gave to real estate values has been enjoyed by sites further away from the line more than along the route itself.

To the South lies Canarsie, which in 1903 was described as a "village on Jamaica Bay in the outskirts of Brooklyn, noted for its fish and clams, from which most of the inhabitants derive their means of living." [1] It could be reached at that time by taking any one of the three elevated lines which ran to East New York, and then changing for the Brooklyn and Rockaway Beach Railway. Only a small number of little homes and fishermen's shacks existed there, although a few hotels or boarding houses were open during the summer months. Between 1903 and 1910, the Broadway elevated line was extended from East New York to Canarsie, and in 1913 through the extension of the Broadway line over the Williamsburgh Bridge, direct connection

[1] Appleton's *Dictionary of Greater New York*, 1903, *loc. cit.*

from Canarsie to Chambers Street, Manhattan was provided. In 1910 over 75 per cent of the land was still vacant. Out of some 1300 buildings in the whole territory, over 950 were one-family houses. Ten years later only 400 more houses had been constructed. It will be interesting to compare the total land values for a number of years:

1910	$6,820,000
1911	7,761,000
1912	7,711,000
1913	7,350,000
1920	7,308,000
1921	7,314,000

Evidently new transit facilities did not awaken any new growth or development here. However, since the war, something seems to have happened. In the attempt to secure cheap housing in the post-war building shortage, there was a rush for all available areas within a five-cent fare zone. Canarsie met this requirement. Since 1921 over 2500 homes have been constructed. This, however, still leaves more than half of the land unimproved. The land values have passed through a marked change in the interim. The figures for 1929 show a value of $19,735,000 for this section, or a gain of 170 per cent over the 1921 figures. No new transit facilities have been provided during this period, except that in 1928, the Canarsie elevated line was given access to 14th Street, Manhattan via the new 14th Street-Eastern line, in addition to the Chambers Street connection which it already had. This latter facility had little to do with the value change, however, for in 1927, before the new line had been completed, the land values were $17,244,000.

Despite these recent gains, however, this district has been extremely backward in its development, for it should be noted that for the last quarter century it has gained less than the average rate of growth for the entire borough. This backward condition is still further emphasized if Canarsie is compared with some adjacent section such as the district south of Vanderveer Park, including Flatlands, and Westminister Heights Park—which like Canarsie in 1910 had over 76 per cent of its land vacant. No rapid transit facilities have been built through the area, but by means of buses and street car lines, access may be had to the Brighton Beach subway, or to the Flatbush Avenue station of the Nostrand Avenue extension of the I. R. T. subway. Less than 25 per cent of the land is now vacant. Land values here have shown an average gain since 1910 of over 400 per cent. Like Canarsie, however, these increases have occurred almost wholly since 1921.

One reason which has been given for this lag in the growth of Canarsie is its sewerage problems. Due to its situation at a low level relative to the sea, engineers have been confronted with difficulties in construction. The result has been that small residences have been about the only type of building which could be erected, most of them being equipped with sanitary cesspool systems. Other sections have consequently met with more favor. It should be reiterated here that transit facilities do not of themselves cause increases in land values; they offer accessibility—which may facilitate such growth, provided the area in question is in all other respects desirable. If such demand is lacking, transit lines will not create value.

The most interesting section for study in Brooklyn for the observation of amazing growths in the value of the land is that whole southern territory which in 1900 was still regarded as the " outskirts " of the city. Since 1905, the average increases have been between 800 and 1000 per cent. This includes the areas known as Bay Ridge, Bath Beach, Bensonhurst, Midwood, Sheepshead Bay and Coney Island.

With the exception of the new Fourth Avenue subway

constructed under the dual contracts in 1915 and extended to Fort Hamilton in 1926, virtually all of the rapid transit systems now serving this area have been extended along the routes of four steam surface railroads which were in existence in 1900 and which carried hundreds of thousands of people daily during the summer to the Coney Island beaches. Under the dual contracts signed in 1913, it was provided that these four railways should be improved and made a part of the existing rapid transit system. Accordingly the new Culver line was placed in operation in 1916 and finally completed through to Coney Island in 1920; the West-End line began service as far as 62nd Street in 1916, with operation to Coney Island in 1917; the Brighton Beach line was opened in 1920; and service on the Sea Beach line to Coney Island was opened in 1915. The greater speed and convenience of travel which this transit improvement afforded came at a time when this whole region was beginning to show signs of development.

Save for Coney Island, proper, which was a favorite beach resort of the City—being only eight and one-half miles from the Battery, the rest of the land through which these steam railroads passed, was little developed in 1905. On Coney Island itself, very much progress had been made. Large hotels of excellent construction, restaurants, concert halls, great rows of bath houses, amusement places, club houses and pavilions lined the beaches. Small homes and cottages were built along streets leading to the beaches. Sea Gate (a part of Coney Island) was a most exclusive residence section.

Bensonhurst was a new settlement which occupied the site of the old Benson farm, and showed signs of being a growing settlement. Bath Beach immediately adjoining on the West was a village of much older character, dating its origin from the old Dutch settlements on Long Island. The land was still largely vacant, however, save for the older residences and the new cottages and summer hotels, which occupied sites near the waterfront. Bay Ridge had become a suburban locality, which, because of its pleasant location and high elevation, was rapidly gaining favor. The Fifth Avenue elevated line served this latter area. Sheepshead Bay was a village to the northeast of Coney Island, and situated on the bay from which it was named. It was scantily built-up with cottages and boarding houses catering to a summer trade. It was especially popular at the time on account of its race course. Midwood, located further inland, nearer the Flatbush section of Brooklyn, had made little progress. In addition to the transit lines mentioned for these areas, they were also served by a large number of electric street car lines, and by ferries.

By 1911, average land values throughout this region, had gained more than 150 per cent, the greater gains, however, coming in the Coney Island area. Then, the realty boom for the entire City came to an end, and values through here slid off from one to ten per cent. Recovery began during the later years of the war, although by 1921 most of the land was worth little more than what it had been a decade before. An exception to this, however, was Coney Island, which in 1921 stood over 100 per cent greater in land values that in 1911. In this small part of this outlying section, some 3,000 new buildings were erected during this period, including a number of flats and apartments, but the majority of them, one and two family houses.

The rest of the vicinity, however, was not lacking in building construction, despite the drop in land values. Over 10,000 new structures were erected during the war period of which approximately three fourths consisted of one and two family dwellings. This development is indicated by the fact that in the Bay Ridge and Bath Beach sections, only 25 per cent of the land was vacant in 1921. In Midwood, Bensonhurst and Sheepshead Bay slightly less than half of the land remained undeveloped.

The great increases in values cited came after 1921. In the short span of years since that time, building construction has proceeded apace. Midwood is now 90 per cent improved. In Bay Ridge less than five per cent of the land remains vacant. Bensonhurst has also made rapid strides forward. About 25 per cent of the Sheepshead Bay area is still unimproved.

The number of buildings in this southern territory of Brooklyn has more than doubled within less than a decade. Over 50,000 new homes were constructed, the greater part of these building operations taking place since 1925. The rapid changes have, of course been reflected in the land values. Because of the increased demands made for land suitable for residential purposes, and for retail sites in these new communities, and the rapidly decreasing supply available, values have since 1921 risen on the average by several hundred per cent. Reference to Table (7) in the appendix will show the extent of the increases.

Brooklyn thus further illustrates the perplexing assortment of changes in land values which seem to occur along rapid transit routes. As in the Bronx, the greatest increases in value took place in the outlying sections of the borough. Where the borough was already well-developed, the only places where large gains were made in the value of the land were at certain centers of concentration. Land along the transit route changed in value in substantial harmony with the whole surrounding territory—evidencing varying effects as the line was followed through different types of sections. Along the Fifth Avenue elevated line for example, in the Prospect Park section, Fifth Avenue has become a valuable retail street and land values have risen measureably. Further south, the line passes Greenwood Cemetery and values have remained depressed. Then, beyond the cemetery, values have shown marked advances. At 38th Street, the elevated line turns off Fifth Avenue into Third Avenue. Along the latter street, there has been evidence of a moderate increase, but along Fifth Avenue, which continues south into the newer developments in Bay Ridge as the leading retail street, the values have mounted over 400 per cent since 1921. It is extremely doubtful that Fifth Avenue might have evidenced any greater increase in value here had the elevated line continued along that street instead of swinging into Third Avenue. Judging from the experiences already observed on other streets adjoining elevated lines, it is quite probable that the growth in value may not have been as great in the latter instance.

The conditions observed in Manhattan, the Bronx and Brooklyn all seem to point to the fact that no definite results in the changes of value of land can be directly attributed to subway and elevated lines, without a consideration of the nature of the vicinity through which they pass. It is in truth a "transit-plus" problem. Queens alone remains for examination of New York City's experiences in land-value growth, relative to its transit lines.

CHAPTER X

Borough of Queens

Queens is the largest borough of Greater New York. Yet, aside from Richmond it has fewer transit lines than any of the other boroughs. As a matter of fact, the rapid transit history of Queens does not begin until 1915.

However, Queens was not without the means of transportation all this time. The Long Island Railroad was built in 1832 and by 1837 had extended from Brooklyn through Queens, and beyond into Nassau County. In 1860, another route to Long Island City was operated from Jamaica. In 1864, a line from Long Island City to Flushing, through Woodside was opened. At the opening of the Twentieth Century, the Long Island Railroad linked together every ward in the borough, provided access to other parts of Long Island, and made direct connection with Brooklyn. In 1905, the first electrification of the railroad was opened to Jamaica. By 1908, the system had been electrified within the borough lines.

Besides these railroad routes, Queens was provided with ferries and with a number of street car lines. As in other boroughs, these latter facilities were chiefly local in character—serving certain local centers or supplementing the existing railroads.

In 1905, Queens was for the greater part, a region of farms—mostly devoted to the production of the vegetables for sale in the city markets. Interspersed here and there, were little villages of suburban homes chief among which were Jamaica, Glendale, Flushing, College Point, Whitestone,

Woodhaven, Richmond Hill, Far Rockaway, Rockaway, Arverne, Laurelton, Queens Village, Rosedale, Hollis, Spring-

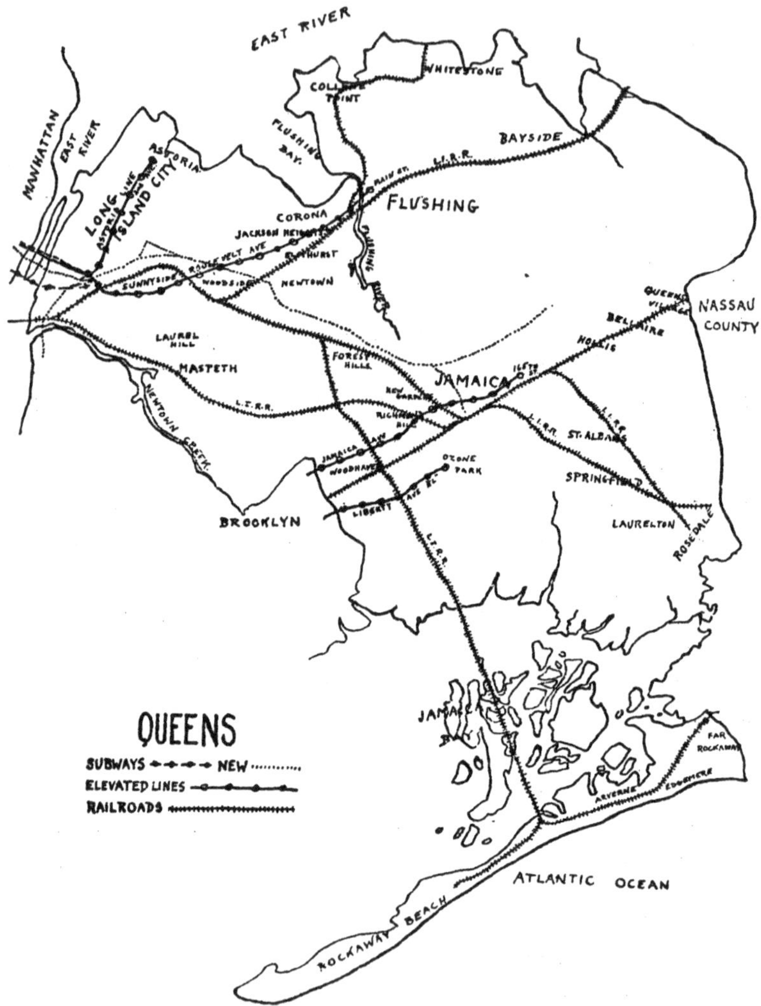

field, Bayside and Little Neck. Long Island City on the East River, opposite Manhattan contained many factories, and adjoining homes were chiefly those of industrial workers.

The population of the entire borough was approximately 200,000 or about five per cent of the population of the Greater City. Today it is more than 15 per cent of the total. The value of the land was about $65,000,000. Today it is $850,000,000. How rapidly did this growth occur? To what extent is it attributable to the extension of the new transit lines into the borough?

The expansion of Queens took place in certain areas while others retained their early characteristics for some time. Long Island City, already the principal industrial center of the borough, received its great stimulus when in 1909, the Queensboro Bridge was opened to vehicular traffic, thus inaugurating the first direct transportation from Queens borough to Manhattan. From that time on, Long Island City has enjoyed an uninterrupted growth. With large plots of land available for factories and warehouses, and within a few minutes run by auto from the offices of companies located in Manhattan, this part of Queens has come to enjoy an enviable position for industrial development. In 1905, the land here, including the section of Astoria, was worth approximately $20,000,000 or about 30 per cent of the value of the whole borough, although in size it is only seven per cent of the area of Queens. In 1910, the land had more than doubled in value, becoming worth $49,529,000; in 1911, $60,141,000, in 1913 $63,349,000. The real estate slump in the rest of the City did not stop this expansion. In 1921 the value of this region had become $72,492,000, which represented almost 25 per cent of the total borough value. Although the rest of the borough was also expanding in value this small area was almost able to keep pace with the other 93 per cent of the land.

During this period, Long Island City was literally being transformed. Big industrial plants erected modern concrete structures. The number of factories doubled—numbering over 400 in 1921. Large warehouses and loft buildings were also constructed.

Meanwhile Queens was getting its first rapid transit lines. Under the Dual contracts of 1913 it was provided that two new elevated lines should be constructed:—one to run along Second Avenue in Long Island City north into Ditmars Avenue, Astoria; the other eastward along Queens Boulevard and Roosevelt Avenue into Corona. Both of these lines terminate in Long Island City at a large junction station—Queensboro Plaza. Provision was further made to link these routes to Manhattan via a tunnel under the East River at 59th Street, Manhattan, connecting there with the new Broadway subway. Another tunnel, the old Steinway tunnel at 42nd Street, was to be reconstructed so that an Interborough subway route from Grand Central in Manhattan might be built to Jackson Avenue in Long Island City and from there extended to the Queensboro Plaza. The arrangements also provided for a connection of the Second Avenue elevated line in Manhattan, across Queensboro Bridge to the Plaza.

In 1915, the Queensboro subway to Jackson Avenue was constructed, and in successive years following this the Queens Plaza station was opened, and the routes were extended to Astoria and Corona. By 1920, the entire system was completed.

Where the new transit system enters Queens along the East River waterfront, there has been little improvement in value. In the district lying between the Newtown Creek and the Queensborough Bridge, the land had already been put to use for industrial purposes long before any transit lines were planned for the borough, and transit could add little to its attractiveness. In fact, in the zone just adjacent to and slightly north of Newtown Creek, land values have actually declined! What has caused this? The main answer to be given is that the Long Island Railroad tunnel to Pennsylvania Station is principally at fault. In 1910, the system of running through trains from Jamaica to Manhattan via the new tunnel to Pennsylvania Station was inaugurated. Before that time, Hunters Point Station in Long Island City was the last stop of the Long Island trains, and passengers then changed for the 34th Street Ferry to Manhattan. This transient population daily passing through this region made property valuable, and land along Jackson Avenue, Borden Avenue and adjoining streets near the river, was the most valuable frontage in Long Island City.

It has already been indicated how in Manhattan the East side of 34th Street has long suffered from the loss of business of the ferry passengers who are now carried by tunnel to the West side. Here is the parallel of this on the Queens side. Values today along the streets mentioned are less than they were before 1910. Although somewhat of a revival has taken place by now, the recovery has not been great enough to carry values back to their early levels. Many vacant buildings and empty stores still serve as monuments to this blow to property values. The new subway has done little to enable the section to recover.

If land north of the bridge and west of the path of the new elevated line to Astoria along Second Avenue is studied it will be seen that in the greater part of this area, as far north as Grand Street, the growth in value of the land was confined to small gains from 1913—the date of the signing of the contracts to build the new transit lines, to 1920, the date of their full completion. However, since this period was a very dull one for real estate activity in general, it would hardly be fair to use this as a basis for judging the results which the transit might have produced. From 1921 to the present, on the other hand, there has been a very active period in the real estate business. In view of this great activity and the results shown for other parts of this borough, the land values of the section referred to have, even in this period, failed to register any extraordinary gains. Some of the water-front property has not changed in value at all. The average increases in value have been between 20 per cent and 150 per cent. Much of this land has been reclaimed from ill-smelling marshy tracts which could not be used until the land was filled in. This was completed within the last decade and values have risen in these parts to the levels already established in the surrounding area. Practically all of this land has been given over to industrial uses.

North of Grand Street the story is quite different. This is Astoria, which had early developed as a suburban community, with charming dwellings lining the waterfront. A ferry to New York, and street car lines had been serving this section. The opening of a through connection to Manhattan by train made the land here, (which was still largely unimproved), much more attractive, and between 1913 and 1929, land values multiplied from three to ten times. Even here, however, a fairly long walk is required between many of the homesites and the transit line.

Queensboro Plaza, of course, formed a concentration point. In 1909, at the time of the opening of the bridge, the land immediately situated around the Plaza district was worth from $20 to $200 a front-foot. By 1921, this land had become worth from $200 to $500 a front-foot. Today the front-foot value ranges from $300 to $1800. From this center, values quickly taper off to less than $150 a front-foot in the nearby vicinity—within a radius of two blocks from the Plaza.

The changes which have occurred in land-values in that part of Long Island City lying to the East of the elevated line running along Second Avenue are responsible for most of the big increases which have been witnessed in this ward in recent years. Yet along the route of the transit line itself, at least as far north as Astoria Avenue, the land has made no marked gains in value. From First Avenue to Ninth Avenue average gains since 1913 have ranged between 100 to 200 per cent along the avenues, and Second Avenue is no exception to this general rule. The largest increases in land value have been registered along the leading business streets—chief among which is Broadway—running perpendicular to Second Avenue. Lots fronting on this street have jumped in value to some 300 to 800 per cent above the 1913 figures. Grand Avenue, parallel to Broadway, has also shown better than average gains. Both of these streets, already the leaders, have been chosen as station sites for the transit line and the passenger traffic through these thoroughfares no doubt enhances their value. Steinway Street, eight blocks east of Second Avenue, has also passed through some unusual value changes since 1913, showing increases varying between 150 and 1000 per cent. In the Astoria district, the blocks surrounding the Ditmars Avenue terminal of the Second Avenue line have become worth from five to ten times more than the neighboring land. This has been caused by the demand for the highly desirable retail frontages within this limited area.

The Queens Boulevard and Roosevelt Avenue arm of the subway into Queens, proceeds as an elevated road into Corona. Needless to say, investments in property through here have become very valuable within a relatively short time. A large percentage of the land which is easily accessible to this transit facility was still cheap, vacant land less than a decade ago. Since that time, there have been large scale operations in improving this land. In 1923 for example, the City Housing Corporation acquired a tract over seventy acres in size adjoining Queens Boulevard between Laurel Hill Avenue and Lincoln Avenue. Both the Bliss Avenue and Lincoln

Avenue stations of the subway serve this section. This raw land was graded, streets and public utilities were put through, and houses were erected to form what is now known as the community of Sunnyside. Queens Boulevard became the business street, providing stores for the community. By 1926 over 600 families were living in this new residential section which three years before had been barren land. This sort of residential growth has spread through this whole area served by the new transit line—including Woodside and Elmhurst. For miles new rows of one-family houses which virtually sprang up over night meet the eye.

Jackson Heights is another region which has made rapid progress. It consists of one hundred city blocks lying between Roosevelt Avenue and Jackson Avenue, and served by the Fisk Avenue, Broadway, 25th Street and Elmhurst Avenue stations of the subway. Since 1920, this part of Queens has gone through a miraculous transformation. On this large acreage has arisen the largest restricted cooperative garden apartment community in the world. Planned under the management of the Queensboro corporation, a complete community of apartments and of private homes of two and three stories, all of distinctive architectural design was the result. Millions of dollars have been expended in the construction of these communities. Since 1921, the land in this latter section has gained in value on the average over 300 per cent in the residential part of the settlement, and from 500 per cent to over 1000 per cent along Queens Boulevard, and Jackson Avenue which have developed as the business streets. In 1928, the extension of the Roosevelt Avenue line into Flushing was made. The line comes to an end at Main Street, Flushing, immediately adjoining the Long Island Railroad station at Flushing, which has been there for years. Since 1921 the land values around this terminus increased in value tenfold. Main Street had always been an important and valuable business street, housing the leading financial and business interests. The land all along Main Street made further substantial gains. Other important arteries radiating out from the location of the station, such as Roosevelt Avenue and Kissena Blvd. rose by large percentages. But all of Flushing has been growing—especially along Broadway and all of the adjacent streets where large elevator apartments have been constructed. Property values here have shown gains commensurate with those experienced by the areas above mentioned. Flushing has been a high-class residential district for years. It was settled in the 17th century by Dutch Colonists and grew slowly as a suburban community on the outskirts of New York. In 1903, the Long Island Railroad provided thirty-four minute service to East 34th Street by means of the 34th Street Ferry. At that time, it was estimated that 19,000 people were living there, and that a fairly large portion of them were daily commuters to the city. Since then, it has become more and more developed. Access to the city on a five-cent fare will probably stimulate further apartment house construction than has already taken place.

Under the 1913 contracts, several other transit lines were provided for Queens. The Myrtle Avenue elevated line of Brooklyn was extended into the Ridgewood section. As has already been mentioned with reference to Brooklyn, this area in Queens also benefited from the new 14th Street Eastern line which was partly constructed along the Queens boundary line. Since 1913, land values have increased between 50 and 200 per cent in parts of this new residential section, evidencing an overflow of the Brooklyn population, and a consequent conversion of vacant land into improved lots. Along Myrtle Avenue and Fresh Pond Road, the land advanced more than 500 per cent in some parts, especially near the stations. West of this region, between the Newtown

Creek and the new elevated line along Roosevelt Avenue and Queens Boulevard, land values have been slow to rise. Great stretches of barren land are still found in parts of this territory and in others, rows of empty buildings stand as evidence of an ill-fated development. The existence of over a thousand acres of cemetery here, has probably helped to discourage growth.

In 1915 the Liberty Avenue line, an extension of the Brooklyn Fulton Street line from Grant Avenue to Lefferts Avenue in Richmond Hill was opened. This passed through an area which at the time was little developed. By 1921, there were but minor increases in value. Today, however, all of the land in this vicinity has become from two to four times as valuable as it was in 1921, due to the big housing development projects which, like in so many parts of Brooklyn and Queens, were launched after the war. On Liberty Avenue itself, which has become a leading retail street, especially west of 100th Street, gains of from 500 to 1000 per cent were made. It is noteworthy, however, that along the course of Liberty Avenue, which extends beyond the end of the elevated road at Lefferts Avenue, this rate of increase has continued undiminished.

The Jamaica Avenue elevated extension beyond Cypress Hills went into service in 1918, to Jamaica. This served such communities as Woodhaven, Richmond Hill and Jamaica, all of which had been long established and fairly well developed by that time. The trolley lines along Jamaica Avenue and the Long Island Railroad were already serving the needs of a large population. The elevated line brought to these sections quick, cheap transit to Brooklyn and Manhattan, and in doing so, attracted a much larger number of people, most of whom came from Brooklyn to live in a more suburban, and less crowded residential area. This movement had already begun before the elevated line was built and each year saw the completion of hundreds of new homes in this expansive tract of land. Therefore, when the elevated line came, a large proportion of the territory which it tapped, especially in the Woodhaven section had already been developed, and as a result the highest gains which the residential land has made since the transit line was built have not been in most cases much over 100 per cent. The buying population which the elevated road has been able to draw into this area, however, has been a most important factor in the growth in value of its principal retail street—Jamaica Avenue, along which the transit line runs. Between Cypress Hills and Elderts Lane, the part of the new elevated spur which lies in Brooklyn, there has been little growth, for the continuity of a retail street has been broken by the existence of a cemetery fronting on the north side of Jamaica Avenue. Crossing the borough line into Queens, this undesirable condition at once disappears, and as the street is followed into Woodhaven, and Richmond Hill, the retail business is found to be very prosperous, enjoying a large patronage drawn from the surrounding residential community which looks to it as practically the only retail shopping district in the neighborhood,—a position which it held for many years when the Jamaica Avenue trolley line was serving these communities. In view of the larger population which has moved into the neighboring environment since the elevated line was built, this street has enjoyed a larger retail trade and has gained in value by 200 to 300 per cent. Beginning with Van Wyck Boulevard in Jamaica, and running east to the last stop of the elevated route at 168th Street, however, the rise of the property values has been enormous, showing increases since 1918 of several hundred per cent all along the avenue, and such unusual gains as those between 160th and 163rd Streets, where land has risen from $550 and $800 a front-foot to $6000 a front-foot in this short period of time.

Large department stores, theaters and high-class retail shops have established themselves along here, and many of the big chain-store systems have chosen this location. The Manhattan and Brooklyn department stores have seen fit to open branch stores in this thriving section. The elevated line brings to these theaters and stores many people who would otherwise have gone into the shopping district of downtown Brooklyn. In fact, it was ever since the construction of this elevated line to Jamaica that the department stores of Broadway, Brooklyn, have experienced their worst falling-off in trade. With the large migration of Brooklyn residents to other parts of Brooklyn more accessible to Fulton Street, coupled with a similar migration of former residents of Brooklyn to Queens, the business of these Broadway stores in Brooklyn, has become less prosperous. To a degree this also applies to certain types of local trade in sections such as East New York, and Cypress Hills in Brooklyn, and even in such promising retail districts as Woodhaven and Richmond Hill, where transit facilities have made easy access either to Jamaica, or to the Fulton Street shopping district in Brooklyn and to this extent serve to draw customers away from the local stores. The result is to shift values upward in these fortunate centers, at the expense of the local retail areas which otherwise might enjoy a greater growth.

There remain for discussion those parts of Queens which have not to date obtained any direct access to the subway and elevated systems of New York City, but which nevertheless compare favorably in their growths in value with those sections which have been more fortunate in this respect. Although a large part of Queens falls into this category, it will suffice to take for illustration, the settlements of St. Albans, Springfield, Rosedale, Hollis, Bellaire and Queens Village.

In 1900, Hollis and Queens Village were small villages several miles apart, separated by hundreds of acres of farm land. A trolley line along Jamaica Avenue connected them with Jamaica. The Long Island Railroad had a station at Queens Village and at Hollis, and a flag station at Bellaire. Springfield and St. Albans, further to the South were also served by the Long Island Railroad. In 1908, these lines were electrified into Brooklyn, and from there, passengers could change for the Interborough subway into Manhattan. In 1910 direct service could be secured to Pennsylvania station over the Woodside tracks and through the newly constructed tunnel to Manhattan.

In 1920, potatoes were still growing on the farms in this part of Queens. The population of the villages had increased; a few more stores were opened on Jamaica Avenue, a few housing developments were started; the Long Island Railroad elevated its tracks onto an embankment and built larger newer stations, but aside from this, all was still much the same. The 1921 tax map of the city still quoted the value of the land in terms of acreage and where block values were indicated, they were placed at from five to twenty dollars a front-foot for most of the land and at twenty-five to thirty-five dollars along Jamaica Avenue.

Then something happened. Store lots on Jamaica Avenue sold as high as $10,000 a lot, or about $400 a front-foot. The average front-foot values along this street became from $160 to $500. Land for residential purposes also increased in value, showing gains of between 200 and 800 per cent in these communities. Building activity ran apace, thousands of new homes being erected each year. Most of these were one-family houses, but a few apartment houses have been erected. The rate of expansion may be judged by comparing the populations of these districts for this period. In 1920, the official census reports placed them as follows:

Hollis, Queens, Bellaire	7,000
Springfield, St. Albans, Rosedale	6,000

The preliminary estimate compiled by the Queens Borough Chamber of Commerce for Queens county [1] places 1930 population in these communities as follows:

Hollis, Queens, Bellaire	52,550
Springfield, St. Albans, Rosedale	22,200

This, compared with the grand total for Queens Borough for these two years: 1920—469,000; 1930—1,098,000 indicates the greater rapidity of growth of these outlying areas during this decade.

It may be said then, that virtually the whole development of these areas has come within the last ten years. Yet no transit lines have been built recently. The new City subway will not quite reach these communities according to present plans, but many civic bodies have petitioned for an extension of this subway into their respective settlements. However, thus far no new routes have been definitely decided upon, so that it might be said that no new transit was either supplied nor contemplated during this period.

What then, brought about this remarkable growth? Was it due to the extension of the Broadway elevated line to Jamaica? Hardly, for the great majority of the residents here commute on the Long Island Railroad, very few of them bothering to take buses or trolley cars to the elevated station in Jamaica.

The reason for this growth is explained in terms of the great post-war demand for housing in any vicinities that were at all accessible. Although the Long Island commutation fare is not cheap, the system provides direct rapid transportation into Jamaica, the Borough Hall district of

[1] Annual estimate of the population of Queens, Queens Borough Chamber of Commerce, February, 1930.

Brooklyn, and mid-town Manhattan—the three great concentration points of New York City, and from its Brooklyn terminal is only ten minutes by subway, from the downtown business district of Manhattan.

Of course, this facility was available for years, but the pressure of demand for residential property in this part of the City did not come until after the World War. Property values did not rise materially until this demand developed, despite the fact that the Long Island trains served this section in 1837 and provided rapid electric service in 1908. Of course, since the population has grown, the number of trains serving these communities have also been increased, thereby adding somewhat to the desirability of the property.

By providing a five-cent fare, a subway extension into these neighborhoods might somewhat enhance the value of the land served by it. The values would probably not mount by very much, however, in the places where whole communities of houses have already been constructed. The greatest enhancements in value have already been secured in the conversion of farm land into residential areas. Except where retail streets will benefit, or where large apartment-house projects can be erected, no different uses will be made of the land if a subway is built, than the sites are put to now. The zoning of these sections is restrictive, making apartment-house construction on any large scale quite improbable. In view of this fact, it seems that whether additional transit facilities are provided in these communities or not, the rate of growth in the value of this property will be very much slower from now on, unless the demands on the part of the growing New York population become so insatiable in quest of residential sites lying within the city limits that rental values will increase measurably throughout the City. Then, of course, zoning laws would probably have to be changed, to facilitate the construction of multiple dwellings, and additional transit would be necessary to physically handle the increasing numbers. Under these circumstances, the value of the land would naturally go to many times over the existing levels. In all probability, however, this condition would first evidence itself among the older small-home districts nearer the centers of business concentration.

From a realty standpoint Queens has been very fortunate in recent years. It had thousands of acres of raw land (situated within relatively short-time traveling distance from the business centers of the City), ripe for development at a time when other parts of the City had reached a stage of congestion. The construction of its transit lines came at a time when they could best facilitate an expansion which it seemed would be inevitable. The results, of course, were that there was a magical transformation of those territories which had been relatively inaccessible before. Where transportation had long existed, the great development projects which were launched called into service these facilities which had for years enjoyed only moderate patronage. The building of new homes and the attraction of hundreds of thousands of new residents within the last decade, have brought into the borough, new stores, churches, schools, theaters and business. The conversion within a quarter century of a large farm area into a major part of the largest city in the world has made the value of Queens land rise over 1000 per cent on the average. It has accomplished in this short space of time what it required many years to achieve in the other boroughs. Hence, the rapidity of its growth.

It is appropriate to add a remark about the borough of Richmond. Like Queens, it was one of the last boroughs to develop. In fact, about half of its land is still unimproved. No transit links have ever connected this borough with others. It has been left more or less isolated. Geographically, it is also isolated, being much more appropriately a part of

New Jersey than of New York. Its distance from Manhattan compared with the other boroughs has made it less popular. Especially is this true of its southern wards, which in a direct line from Wall Street are further from Manhattan than the most westerly part of Queens.

Still, Richmond has developed as a residential borough with some 40,000 homes, and a population exceeding 150,000. With the exception of Queens, it has evidenced a greater percentage gain in land values than any other borough—showing a rise of almost 700 per cent since 1905. This huge gain, of course, represents the conversion of raw land into a finished residential community. The greater part of this increase has occurred, as in Queens, within the last decade. Despite the lack of transit, the overflow of population seeking homes came into Richmond, and as in every borough having large vacant areas, land values rose by several hundred per cent. Undoubtedly, with this great demand for homesites, Richmond would have experienced even greater growth, had it been provided with rapid transit to the other boroughs. It is significant, however, that these large gains were made in spite of the absence of such routes.

CHAPTER XI

Conclusions

It appears that land values are phenomena, very erratic in character, not conforming to any set rules or orderly arrangements, but rather evidencing a restlessness and inconstancy as capricious at times as the winds. They depend in final analysis upon the degree of conflicting demands existent, for locations limited in extent. These demands for land in specific areas are with reference to certain uses to which the land is to be put. The decision concerning the desirability or suitability of a site for some particular employment will be affected by an enormous complexity of influences, including such considerations as legal restrictions, environmental conditions, existence of established centers, past records of stability or growth in values, size or extent, and shape of the area in question, and accessibility. To this must be added many psychological situations such as desires to "follow the leader" in a trade, mere whims or fancies to be different, or to go elsewhere because of being "bored" with another location, speculative fervor, etc. The importance of such influences varies under different circumstances. As has been aptly said by Mr. Hurd:[1] "Change is a law of life, and as long as human activity continues to alter the conditions of city life and human tastes, prejudices, fashions, habits and customs continue to vary, city structure and values will shift and change . . ." Roughly, the people who choose property, may be divided into two classes—those who select it for

[1] *Principles of City Land Values*, Richard M. Hurd, 1905, p. 159.

service in such a form that it will contribute directly toward a satisfaction of their wants as consumers, and those who select it as a site necessary for some productive operation. The first group choose such areas as will give them the greatest amount of satisfaction as a site, usually, for a residence, This applies both to those who buy a home, and to those who rent an apartment. Their selection will depend upon the degree of comfort and convenience, which they will secure in comparison with any other location. The second group determine the place of choice from the point of view of the situation which will best contribute toward the business-getting or profit-making capacities of the concerns involved. In both cases, the item of cost is a large factor. In the first case, the amount of satisfaction derived, will depend materially upon how expensive it is to obtain such pleasure, and how capable the individual is of meeting this expenditure. In the second case the size of the profit anticipated, will considerably influence the willingness to pay for the desired location.

Both groups very often conflict with one another in the choice of an identical site. In such situations, pleasure coupled with ability to pay for it, is matched against business-getting ability and profit possibilities. The stronger group is triumphant, and this has usually been the latter group.

Land values will therefore show a tendency to vary, whenever either one of these groups makes new choices. Such new choices, may, as has been stated, arise out of many different circumstances. The area which is singled out in such choice-making is usually favorably affected in value, the degree depending upon the potency of the demand.

It has been said that ample transit facilities, the evidence that certain types of business activities are to stay in a locality, and efforts of other business tenants to enter the same neighborhood, are the three prime factors in making certain locations valuable in New York City. Whenever these sites are wanted by operators for still higher yielding improvements, land prices naturally rise. The section which experiences a loss of favor for a certain use, may or may not suffer a loss in value, depending upon whether or not it falls heir to a new series of demands for a different use. If this new use is more profitable, or gives more satisfaction to those who are able to pay for it than did the former use, the value of the land in all probability will rise.

New York City has in the last quarter century gained in land values by about five billion dollars. Of this increase, almost half has occurred in Manhattan, and approximately half of this amount, or one and a quarter billions of dollars has been added to the value of the small financial district south of Fulton Street, and the midtown zone including Pennsylvania and Grand Central terminals, and Times Square. Manhattan has shown greater growth in value in terms of dollars than have any of the other larger boroughs. But, it must be remembered that in 1905 Manhattan was more than three times as great in value as all of the other boroughs put together. When this is considered, it will be seen that the increase in value of an average investment in Manhattan has been much less relative to an investment of similar size in a borough such as Queens. But this is a mere vague generalization. An investment in Manhattan in the Grand Central zone has multiplied in value many times since 1905, whereas land in the lower East side, or along Broadway south of 14th Street has actually declined. Similarly, a gain of more than 1000 per cent was made in Jamaica in this period whereas Hunters Point has offered little promise.

Furthermore, the huge percentage gains registered for the outlying territories are to be accounted for chiefly by the fact that the land has been converted from farm use into urban use. From the standpoint of cost of such conversion alone, an acre of land worth $2,000 should become worth at least $10,000 on the basis of development costs of from $500 to $1,000 a lot. Once the initial stage has been passed, however, the rate of growth in the land value becomes very much less, whether additional transit facilities are made available or not, unless the effect is to cause residential land to be diverted into business use. In the latter case, of course, the degree of value increase of the land will depend upon the profitableness of the business which can use it to advantage.

Another factor which must not be overlooked in the unusual expansion of real estate values in general, since the War, is the change which has occurred in the dollar value. Unlike commodity prices, real estate does not rapidly rise and fall in value when there are variations in the credit and currency conditions. There appears to be a lag, probably caused by the slow volume of turnover of title or of control through leases of such property. Nevertheless, there is ultimately a reflection in capital values, of changes in the general level of commodity prices, or in other words, of changes in the purchasing power of the dollar. That is, if there has been no change in the dollar value of property since 1913, it has actually declined in value relative to other things, since the dollar of today will buy less than the dollar of 1913 could buy. Therefore, a part of the increase in the value of New York City property since the War is to be considered as due to a change in the purchasing power of the dollar. Using a general index of the purchasing power of the dollar in terms of the 1913 dollar, in comparison with actual dollar value, average land values in Manhattan appear to have shown little increase since 1913, and for the other boroughs the rates of increase appear considerably lessened.

Only if these value levels continue to be maintained as commodity prices drop, and the purchasing power of the dollar comes back more closely to the pre-War level, can they be considered as permanent gains. (See Chart III in the Appendix).

Now what roles do transit facilities play in all of this fluctuation of land values? As was indicated previously, their influences have not seemed to display any uniformity in New York City. They have not caused a super-growth in values in the whole City. The land adjoining them has tended to reflect the changes that were going on in the districts through which they have passed. They have hastened developments which have occurred in some parts of the City.

A glance at the maps may recall to the reader the varied conditions of land-value changes which have been experienced along or near transit arteries in the City. In some cases, increases have been found to exceed 1000 per cent. In others, on the other hand, actual losses have been experienced so that in not a few localities the value today is less than that which prevailed before subways were known in New York City. Moreover, in a large number of areas there has been a kind of indifference to the presence of transit facilities, the value of land along such routes behaving in no different manner than that for an entire section of which it is a part.

Alluding to some of the points which have already been brought forward, the following brief summary may be made in conclusion: It seems clear that:

(1) The building of subways in New York has been accompanied by shifts in land values from one part of the City to another. Shifts in location are apt to be accelerated by transit lines running in the same direction as the shift is going. This operates to transfer values rather than to increase values. To the extent that this newer transportation draws the activities of

the people into different directions, it tends to affect adversely the value of plots in those locations which had depended on existing transportation.

(2) Certain influences upon land values have frequently caused decreases which the opening up of new transit facilities was unable to overcome. In such cases, it is questionable to assert the existence of a resulting local benefit.

(3) Certain centers of concentration tend to be formed in a city, and have the effect of drawing into them the greater part of the business activity of the surrounding territory. Where transit facilities serve to direct the streams of population into those centers, the effect is to enhance the value of such centers, at the expense of the other areas which such transit lines tap.

(4) Neighborhoods already clearly marked in their development for certain characteristic uses, usually fail to show any noteworthy increase in land values when transit lines are extended to them, provided, after the transit line has been opened, the areas continue to be employed for these same uses. Especially is this true in such places as long established industrial regions which have been selected primarily because of their desirable location along water-fronts and railroad freight spurs, and where not much importance is attached to improved accessibility to other parts of the city.

(5) In districts already supplied with a number of transit facilities, the addition of another line does not afford as much possibility of a stimulus to realty growth as would be the case in an area never supplied with transit. An exception to this may occur where the former area has developed as an important concentration center.

(6) Land along the course of transit routes shows changes in values which reflect the character of growth of the whole area through which these lines pass—rising measurably in regions that show rapid expansion, changing little in somewhat "settled" areas, and dropping in those regions which undergo a general decline.

(7) The usual practice which has been followed, of selecting the old main streets of given localities through which the transit line is constructed as station sites, has caused these thoroughfares to assume unusual values compared with the rest of the surrounding blocks. Where, as it has occasionally occurred, these streets were not so chosen, it has taken relatively longer for the newer street which was favored to develop as an important business thoroughfare, and as a consequence, the old main road has gradually shown a decline.

(8) Transit lines which have become obsolete, such as certain elevated spurs, tend to keep down land values in sections which would otherwise rise. The immediate results which follow such construction may consist in the fact that lots in the adjoining territory will rise in value because of the augmented demand for land which has become more accessible. Experience has shown, however, that on streets through which such lines have been built there has usually been somewhat of a retarding effect upon future growth when compared with neighboring properties not so encumbered.

(9) Although new sections may be developed profitably only after rapid transit facilities have been extended to them, a great part of the resultant large increase in values arises out of subdividing operations. The

rise in land values which occurs after the opening of new transit lines in regions where the movement of population has preceded the construction of the line, is usually less than where the population movement follows such construction.

(10) A development, stimulating demand for a certain locality, may have the effect of increasing land values. This may take place during the construction of a transit line, directly after its opening, or many years after it has served the area, or it may even occur in a territory not supplied with transit facilities at all, but otherwise accessible from regions so supplied.

(11) Rather than to be considered a cause of land value changes, a transit facility should more properly be regarded as a construction which permits or facilitates, under certain circumstances, an emergence of land values, the values being determined largely by other factors.

(12) Effects of rapid transit construction cannot be assumed to be uniform, and therefore no policy of special assessments can be equitably applied if it seeks to make a mechanical levy according to some fixed formula for an area supposedly affected by new transit lines.

In view of the foregoing considerations, it is scarcely possible for the experience of New York to lend support to the statement which says: "That local benefit arises from urban transportation systems is so indisputable as not to warrant further argument or illustration." [1]

[1] *Subway Advisory Commission of Chicago*, Report of 1926.

APPENDIX A

A Possible Alternative to Special Assessments

Although it has been the main purpose of this paper to trace the course of land values in New York City, especially with respect to increases in transit facilities, and to show from the data so presented the undesirability of the use of a common system of special assessments as a means of financing such extensions, it may not be inappropriate at this point to comment upon the possible alternatives which might be used in financing projects of this kind.

As has been evidenced in the foregoing data, the behavior of values of land adjacent to subway lines, has been extremely variant. It was found that it was an error to proceed under the assumption that all land so situated will unquestionably receive great benefits in the form of value increases. Nevertheless, it was also discovered that in certain sections there was a multiplication of values many times over the original figures, which in part was possible only because of the existence of the transit facilities in the designated areas. It is also agreed that much of this value increase is attributable to developments of a social character rather than to the private initiative on the part of the property owners. Where the latter condition holds, it appears equitable for the municipality to share in part of this more or less socially created gain.

How then, might this end be attained without resort to an arbitrary system of levying special assessments upon property owners? A possible alternative is offered in the form of an increment tax on land values.[1] This might be a tax of a definite

[1] A discussion of this type of levy will be found in Seligman, E. R. A., *Studies in Public Finance*, pp. 267-277, "Reform of Municipal Taxation," New York, 1925.

percentage—say five or ten per cent upon the increased value of land in the City which becomes manifest from year to year. Instead of attempting to assume a growth in value which some local improvement may create, this levy would be made against actual growths in value which have occurred from year to year. The defense for such a tax would be on the grounds that social developments have in part been responsible for the increase in land value and that the owner should in justice contribute a small part of this increase for the further improvement of the City. In the event that the land should fall in value, no further taxes of this kind would have to be paid until the value of the land rose above its previous highest value.

The arrangement might be as follows: The City could authorize construction of transit facilities as its needs require, and issue bonds which might be retired on a sinking fund basis. During the life of these bonds, a sinking fund could be set up from funds collected as a tax upon the annual increments in land value which the assessed valuations show. The test for the justification of these increased valuations would be the same as at present. Hearings would be held at which protests would be considered, and decisions handed down, which would establish the new value levels of the property. These new valuations would then act as the basis for the ordinary real estate tax the following year. In addition, however, an established percentage, say ten per cent of the *land value increment* over the preceding year, would have to be paid by the property owner. It would be levied without reference to any particular special benefit enjoyed. This latter payment would be used to build up the sinking fund to retire the bonds. Interest on the outstanding bonds could be paid out of general taxes. The burden of this payment out of general taxes would then gradually diminish as the principal was retired with the sinking fund money.

Inasmuch as the City would continue to expand the transit arteries when required by its general growth, this land-increment tax might be made a permanent levy, upon all land in the

City. This recommendation is offered not only with reference to transit construction, for the same plan is applicable to the financing of all public improvements. The properties would then bear the burden of such construction costs in proportion to the gains which they experienced, out of the general growth of the City. The landowner would bear the burden of the tax, but he would also enjoy the increased values. It may be possible partly to capitalize this tax and so to discount the present value of the land. This would tend to place the future burdens of the tax upon the present owner in the event that he should wish to sell his land. However, a little reflection would soon reveal the fact that not all of such taxation could be capitalized. Since the future growth in value of the property is an unknown quantity, it would be impossible to calculate at the present time what the future burdens of the increment tax would be. At best, one could only hazard a guess.

Whether we adhere to the erroneous theory that all land values in the City will benefit from transit extensions, or accept the more correct interpretation, that influences upon values of land proximate to such transit lines are by no means uniform, the use of an increment tax on land can be defended on either ground. For, if all land is benefited, then all land ought to share in the increment tax, while if only some lands rise in value, and others fall, in spite of subway or elevated construction (as has been demonstrated) then only those lands which rise will bear the burden of the additional taxation. If the officials of the City are not too extravagant or too hasty in the plans for construction of new public works of this kind, a moderate rate, amounting to a very small percentage of the full value of the property could be levied upon the land-value increment, and thus continually provide adequate funds for needed improvements.

If the experience of New York in land-value growth in the last quarter century can be taken as a guide, and if the expansions in land value in the last two years are regarded as unusual, it might be said that a growth of at least two-thirds of one per cent annually in land values might be conservatively expected. On the basis of this assumption, and using the total value of taxable property in New York City in 1927 as a basis for calculation, the annual increment of land should be approximately $200,000,000. If a ten per cent increment tax were levied upon this, it would yield a revenue of $20,000,000, and if this yield continued on an average uniformly for the next thirty years the entire cost of the new $600,000,000 subway could be so defrayed. As a matter of fact, however, the actual gains in land values from 1926 to 1927 were far in excess of this conservatively estimated figure. Since 1927, the gains have been even greater. Taxable land from 1926 to 1927 showed a gain in value of $913,715,815 for New York City. A ten per cent tax levied upon the gain would amount to over $91,000,000 and would permit a complete retiring of the cost of construction of the subway in from five to ten years. If this is considered to be at too rapid a rate, the tax percentage figure might be lowered accordingly.

The discussion here presented has been directed to those who favor a pay-as-you-go policy of financing public improvements. No attempt has been made to discuss the merits or defects of short *vs.* long time financing. The goal has rather been to indicate an alternative to the use of special assessments as they are commonly levied, in the form of another variety of relatively short time financing procedure. We believe that this recommendation provides for a more equitable arrangement in view of the results which have been disclosed in this study.

APPENDIX B

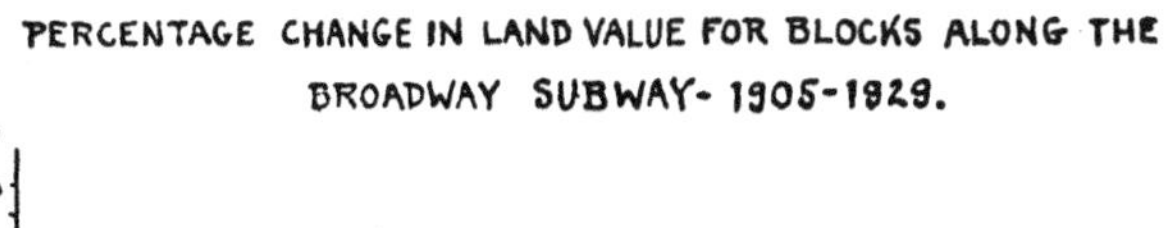

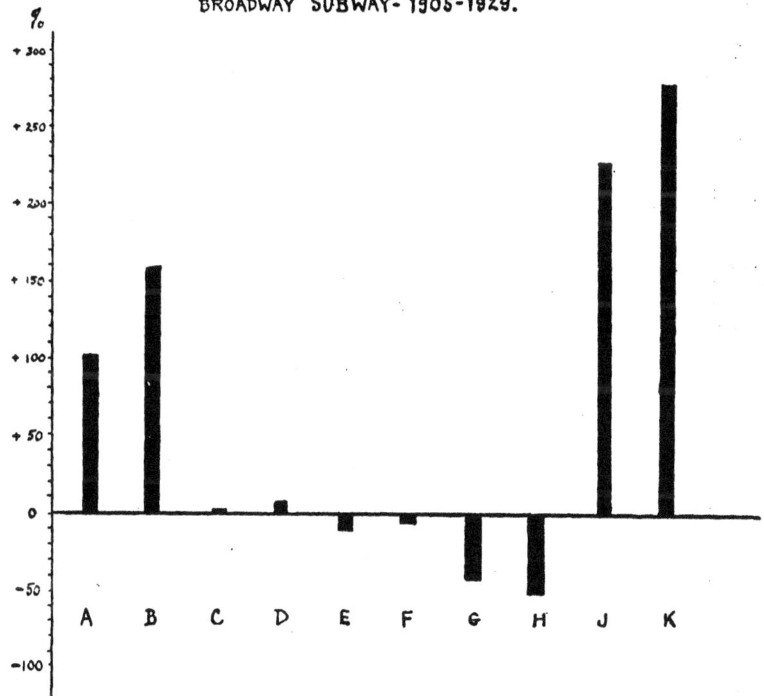

LOCATION OF ABOVE BLOCKS FRONTING ON BROADWAY

- A. LIBERTY TO CORTLANDT STREETS
- B. DEY TO FULTON
- C. READE TO DUANE, WEST
- D. READE TO DUANE, EAST
- E. THOMAS TO WORTH, WEST
- F. THOMAS TO WORTH, EAST
- G HOWARD TO GRAND
- H GRAND TO BROOME
- J 41st TO 42ND STREETS
- K 43RD TO 44TH STREETS

CHART I

PERCENTAGE CHANGE IN LAND VALUE ALONG THE LEXINGTON AVE SUBWAY
1905 - 1929

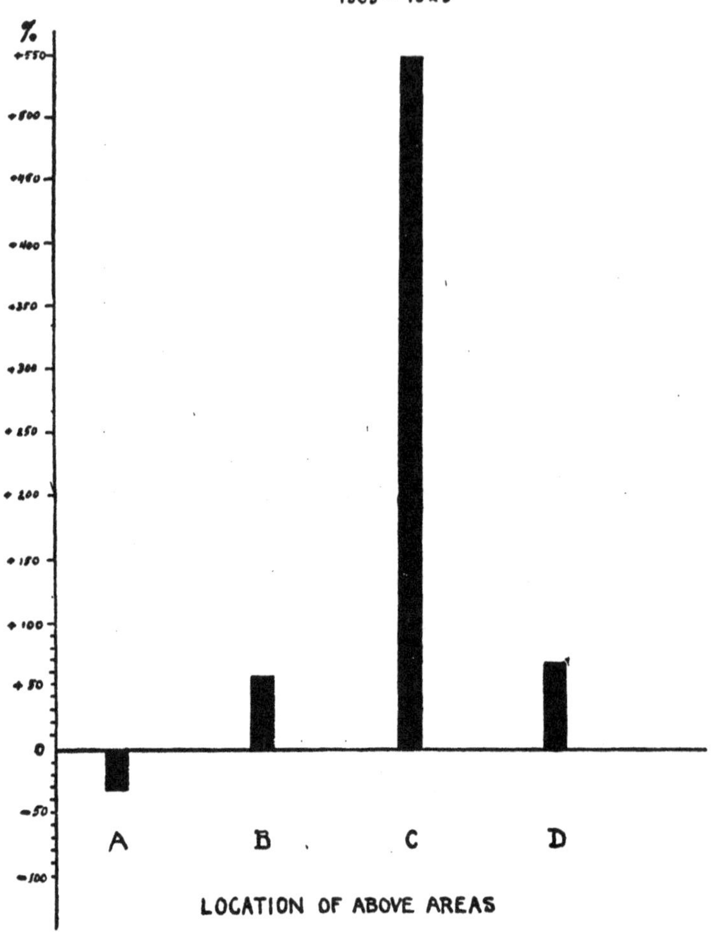

A. FROM E. 3RD. TO E 10TH STS ALONG LAFAYETTE ST.

B. FROM E 15TH. TO E. 17TH STS EAST SIDE OF PARK AVE

C. FROM E 49TH TO E 53RD. STS. ALONG LEXINGTON AVE

D. FROM E. 121ST TO E. 124TH STS. ALONG LEXINGTON AVE.

CHART II

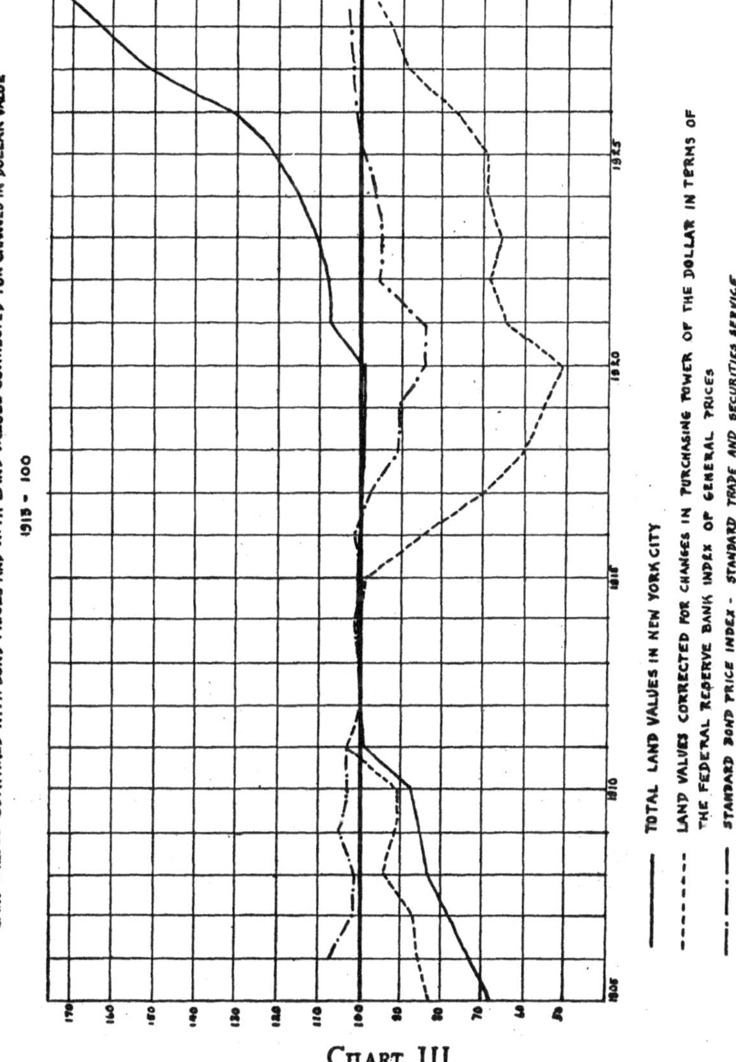
LAND VALUES COMPARED WITH BOND PRICES AND WITH LAND VALUES CORRECTED FOR CHANGES IN DOLLAR VALUE
1915 = 100
170
160
150
140
130
120
110
100
90
80
70
60
50
1906
1910
1915
1920
1925
TOTAL LAND VALUES IN NEW YORK CITY
LAND VALUES CORRECTED FOR CHANGES IN PURCHASING POWER OF THE DOLLAR IN TERMS OF THE FEDERAL RESERVE BANK INDEX OF GENERAL PRICES
STANDARD BOND PRICE INDEX - STANDARD TRADE AND SECURITIES SERVICE

CHART III

APPENDIX C

TABLE 1

ASSESSED VALUES OF TAXABLE LAND FOR ALL BOROUGHS, 1905-1929

Year	Manhattan	Bronx	Brooklyn	Queens	Richmond	All Boroughs
1905..	$2,439,500,000	$175,000,000	$406,000,000	$68,000,000	$19,300,000	$3,107,800,000*
1906..	2,600,140,211	208,970,612	456,313,602	81,270,450	20,538,871	3,367,233,746
1907..	2,707,862,301	216,060,946	485,913,085	123,585,700	25,471,922	3,558,893,954
1908..	2,807,194,281	242,925,919	576,647,240	182,629,206	33,768,951	3,843,165,597
1909..	2,829,746,871	251,690,025	584,521,230	185,899,546	33,869,535	3,885,727,207
1910..	2,905,201,140	265,774,738	596,150,739	200,180,317	33,822,717	4,001,129,651
1911..	3,114,812,658	330,679,808	794,148,607	276,089,172	40,195,031	4,555,929,277
1912..	3,127,852,473	332,945,009	786,159,510	277,644,346	38,756,176	4,563,357,514
1913..	3,155,389,410	332,354,808	782,660,179	280,223,990	40,263,963	4,590,892,350
1914..	3,161,949,660	336,116,060	783,859,159	280,678,120	40,249,108	4,602,852,107
1915..	3,184,441,505	345,712,366	788,155,904	283,983,456	41,121,545	4,643,414,776
1916..	3,133,955,156	350,506,531	795,747,721	289,994,635	41,600,790	4,611,804,833
1917..	3,067,358,846	352,174,951	807,044,424	292,756,798	42,398,585	4,561,733,604
1918..	3,047,602,396	351,455,656	808,696,350	296,461,660	46,261,355	4,550,477,417
1919..	3,033,394,246	351,338,666	816,123,331	297,039,420	52,765,720	4,550,661,383
1920..	3,061,515,951	356,334,831	834,470,621	303,094,525	50,804,370	4,606,220,298
1921..	3,295,207,233	364,614,521	892,559,011	309,174,600	58,499,355	4,920,054,720
1922.	3,315,723,250	366,880,531	914,608,516	318,944,950	59,843,835	4,976,001,082
1923..	3,352,334,985	389,353,266	934,823,526	342,212,360	66,267,065	5,084,991,202
1924..	3,459,593,365	399,780,185	985,872,986	393,736,265	72,674,095	5,311,656,896
1925..	3,571,158,945	411,430,479	1,061,676,391	439,579,570	77,873,560	5,561,718,945
1926..	3,749,159,930	432,043,014	1,234,517,520	564,187,955	88,723,320	6,068,631,739
1927..	4,166,877,955	519,007,944	1,470,434,390	688,911,700	137,115,565	6,982,347,554
1928..	4,438,318,085	601,616,529	1,569,040,085	776,772,380	143,810,030	7,529,557,109
1929..	4,765,047,235	658,412,949	1,632,198,560	850,428,000	150,567,780	8,056,654,524

* 1905 values are estimated.

Data for this table were obtained from the Annual Reports of the Commissioners of Taxes and Assessments of the City of New York and from the Records of the Department of Taxes and Assessments.

TABLE 2*

PERCENTAGE CHANGE IN LAND VALUES OF NEW YORK CITY—1905-1929

Boroughs	% Increase 1905–1911	% Increase 1911–1915	% Increase 1915–1919	% Increase 1919–1929	% Increase 1905–1929
Manhattan	27.6	2.2	†—4.7	57.1	95.2
Bronx	89.1	4.5	1.4	87.4	276.0
Brooklyn	95.5	†—.7	3.5	100.0	301.9
Queens	305.8	2.9	4.5	186.1	1150.0
Richmond	110.5	2.5	2.9	184.9	700.0
All Boroughs.	46.5	1.9	†—1.9	77.0	159.2

* Based upon preceding table.

† Indicates decrease.

TABLE 3

INCREASE IN VALUE OF LAND IN NEW YORK CITY—1905-1929

Boroughs	Increase in Value in Dollars—1905–1929	Percentage of Total Increase for All Boroughs
Manhattan	$2,325,547,235	47.0
Bronx	483,412,949	9.7
Brooklyn	1,226,198,560	24.8
Queens	782,428,000	15.8
Richmond	131,267,780	2.7
All Boroughs	$4.948,854,524	100.0

Data for the following table were compiled directly from the record books in the office of the Department of Taxes and Assessments in Manhattan. Assessed valuations for each individual block were obtained for the years 1905, 1913, 1921, 1927 and 1929. In a great many cases, changes were made in dimensions of blocks where street alterations took place. Where possible, corrections were made in the value of the blocks, to allow for such changes in size. Where the alteration was too sweeping, the entire block was dropped out. Also, all blocks containing property assessed as " Real Estate of Corporations " have been omitted, as well as all piers, bulkheads and land under water. Inasmuch as changes were made in exemptions of property in these blocks, between 1905 and 1929, values given for taxable land were not strictly comparable for each year, unless corrections were made for such variations. The present study was begun in 1927 and therefore that year was used as a base in the adjustment of these exemption values. The exempt list for that year was made the standard, and all lots on that list, (and therefore left out of the assessed values for such blocks in which these lots were located in 1927) were subtracted from the appropriate blocks in the other years, if these lots did not appear on the exempt lists of those years. Similarly, all lots appearing in the exempt lists of other years, but not in the 1927 exempt list, were added back to the assessed valuations of those years. In this way, all blocks for all years were brought down to a comparable basis. The same was later done with 1929, thus adjusting all years with 1927 as the basic year. Inasmuch as no significance has been attached in this study to changes which have specifically occurred between 1927 and 1929, the former year has been omitted in the following table. Figures which are presented here are the final adjusted values for selected blocks in Manhattan for 1905, 1913, 1921 and 1929 —giving intervals of eight years.

TABLE 4

Final Complete Corrected Assessed Valuations of Land by Blocks for Manhattan

(000 omitted)

I. The Downtown Business Area

A. The Wall Street District (Land South of Fulton Street)

*Blocks**	*1905*	*1913*	*1921*	*1929*	*Blocks*	*1905*	*1913*	*1921*	*1929*
4	$ 911	$1265	$1675	$1678	45	5068	7955	9145	9155
7	599	793	1121	1135	46	10707	13590	15185	15455
8	924	1232	1810	1968	47	8365	11000	14000	14000
9	2577	3125	3916	4014	48	7165	8630	9750	9750
11	4453	5275	6299	7204	51	773	1977	2795	3190
14	960	1199	1857	1805	52	1002	1171	1185	1253
15	1070	2105	3491	3439	53	535	902	1156	1331
17	933	1450	2004	2004	54	783	1003	1299	1329
18	734	1257	1752	1811	55	453	1036	1275	1432
19	486	814	1069	1079	56	636	1458	1425	1438
20	3391	3670	4665	5970	58	2050	2256	2099	2280
21	5865	7575	8875	9490	59	1320	1557	1590	1768
22	9025	10130	11535	11850	60	1958	2474	2599	2695
23	17198	21050	21675	23765	62	6069	9000	10290	12170
24	5263	6519	7935	7955	63	5368	8490	8885	9395
25	6239	7157	9332	9628	64	7039	8734	8869	9617
26	12579	13195	15635	16800	65	4308	6195	6345	6380
27	7951	8642	9935	10825	66	3872	4517	4815	5400
28	1583	1965	2582	2843	67	3065	4972	5695	6238
29	3718	4642	6976	7709	68	2595	3652	4189	5198
31	1189	1345	2051	2086	69	1126	1677	1890	2211
33	1142	1195	1765	1793	70	683	945	1054	1053
34	479	542	800	639	71	501	680	833	844
35	1032	1173	1680	1701	72	581	720	870	875
37	1130	1420	1888	2020	74	904	1131	1114	1127
38	1225	1252	1901	1978	75	1037	1294	1459	1546
39	1228	1525	2112	2168	76	948	1204	1369	1442
40	6617	7980	8848	9855	78	2841	4583	5918	6329
41	2140	2800	3620	3620	79	5079	7665	7945	7960
42	2035	3288	4115	4145	80	2996	5961	7655	7735
44	6396	7605	9065	9800	82	755	983	1004	1092

* Block numbers refer to the Official City numbering system of blocks. By consulting any of the Land Value Map books of New York City, the exact location of each may therefore be obtained.

B. From Fulton Street, North to Grand Street

Blocks	1905	1913	1921	1929
83	$ 477	$ 631	$ 568	$ 753
84	1299	1494	1578	2220
88	3808	5390	5860	6210
89	3588	4525	5085	5055
90	4767	5910	6635	6770
91	1371	1891	2145	2287
93	1128	1609	1849	2208
94	848	1055	1185	1311
95	872	1034	1030	1112
97	666	843	893	963
98	766	1127	1137	1104
99	996	1289	1367	1394
100	818	1155	1217	1277
101	3713	4833	5023	4990
102	1635	2170	2641	2628
103	946	1276	1270	1324
104	676	1040	1050	1147
105	358	528	487	533
106	352	436	409	417
107	474	581	606	637
108	295	379	382	367
109	193	245	234	234
110	425	546	539	544
111	480	548	500	499
112	447	594	551	580
114	505	667	689	723
115	243	261	229	237
116	496	591	553	562
117	742	903	856	907
118	597	723	783	807
119	1045	1306	1416	1584
120	638	903	905	918
123	2855	4057	5145	4830
124	2959	3463	3927	4016
127	890	1088	1153	1327
128	915	1059	1127	1399
129	748	970	1015	1233
131	823	1067	1080	1434
132	719	795	879	946
134	3404	4059	4243	4388
135	3487	4286	4311	4696
137	1037	1108	1188	1267
138	992	1090	1154	1530
139	1143	1358	1544	1937
140	887	985	1234	1311
141	709	934	1076	1161
142	765	899	1004	1505
143	673	803	878	984
144	1305	1448	1482	1854
149	2768	3149	2985	3060
150	2733	2902	2770	2792
151	$2654	$2513	$2396	$2406
152	2842	2615	2440	2535
154	2173	2529	2341	2337
156	1814	2037	1868	1868
157	1971	1905	1853	1856
159	1350	1475	905	935
161	1097	1307	1322	1480
162	813	959	874	993
163	559	667	656	672
164	483	608	618	708
167	852	1473	1451	1451
170	2497	2517	2460	2475
171	1772	1889	1833	1841
172	1596	1771	1905	1917
173	3119	2819	2474	2660
174	2634	2478	2111	2123
175	2413	2271	1826	1856
180	535	664	793	876
181	590	699	682	801
182	678	905	948	1535
183	620	904	901	1355
185	541	785	779	1007
186	524	737	704	977
187	544	691	633	796
188	461	595	584	650
193	2222	2040	1519	1527
194	1759	1612	1182	1182
195	1663	1616	1412	1438
196	1828	1709	1427	1471
199	677	712	666	676
200	571	602	544	563
201	497	561	542	572
202	769	972	881	954
206	446	529	456	492
210	1030	1061	1304	758
211	636	709	500	514
214	359	387	399	467
215	410	493	481	552
216	612	801	738	944
217	525	631	652	772
218	497	654	594	715
219	372	478	447	503
221	379	447	437	690
223	474	596	537	697
224	492	604	514	737
226	447	461	499	767
228	625	728	518	538
229	803	860	634	676
230	981	1000	672	704
231	2948	2432	1807	1816
232	1646	1445	981	987

Blocks	1905	1913	1921	1929
235	$ 404	$462	$439	$478
236	404	503	456	458
237	559	688	620	626
238	523	656	601	606
239	659	914	825	930
243	435	475	400	445
244	201	195	166	167
245	296	428	319	325
246	320	430	352	352
247	270	335	307	314
248	498	601	508	524
250	522	654	522	620
251	434	463	381	388
252	487	549	446	469
253	917	1009	823	932
255	689	764	576	576
256	317	420	312	312
257	429	552	390	390
258	481	575	439	440
259	262	372	291	287
260	323	447	346	349
261	629	749	442	593
263	398	624	440	440
264	693	1094	1048	1048
265	673	817	550	552
266	802	963	693	704
267	658	758	511	507
268	698	722	571	572
269	1109	1269	1015	1027
270	817	993	824	839
271	1021	1190	915	935

Blocks	1905	1913	1921	1929
272	$860	$948	$683	$683
273	598	663	516	623
276	817	840	685	700
277	866	897	713	713
278	744	788	726	762
279	646	709	670	780
280	909	1089	975	1223
283	1434	1597	1575	1577
285	720	839	768	750
286	1119	1181	997	997
287	544	560	475	486
288	472	489	355	353
289	960	1021	1221	1398
294	538	591	701	735
297	655	773	731	801
298	685	704	673	834
299	630	716	838	929
300	600	702	951	955
301	662	565	761	828
304	943	1078	961	1018
306	847	966	982	1080
307	748	829	905	1099
308	732	848	808	1000
309	502	583	516	599
310	711	860	781	847
311	425	474	445	506
312	786	904	752	804
313	713	872	787	832
314	542	636	596	616
315	560	635	491	500

C. From Grand Street, North to 14th Street

(1) East of the Bowery and Third Avenue

Blocks	1905	1913	1921	1929
321	358	479	284	331
322	235	331	166	168
323	485	649	474	474
324	397	524	378	416
325	410	515	345	361
326	704	753	440	440
328	764	1000	620	627
329	663	867	545	564
330	862	1068	655	655
331	825	881	622	610
332	485	505	369	369
333	836	1093	735	763
334	973	1156	799	839
335	884	1093	737	764
336	868	873	634	641
337	444	442	304	307
338	1032	1294	941	1015
339	1178	1373	964	1108

Blocks	1905	1913	1921	1929
341	822	943	642	696
343	1020	1181	855	935
344	1033	1244	911	1042
345	1089	1312	953	1014
346	957	1261	1101	1258
348	1174	1779	1652	2279
349	1124	1528	1284	1650
350	1170	1521	1139	1441
351	1040	1333	1127	1370
353	1114	1649	1692	2721
354	1288	1709	1336	1552
355	922	1230	901	998
356	509	604	407	423
357	898	774	572	578
358	388	404	352	373
360	599	722	582	591
361	275	320	331	328
363	479	577	449	455

Blocks	*1905*	*1913*	*1921*	*1929*	*Blocks*	*1905*	*1913*	*1921*	*1929*
371	$206	$242	$190	$187	423	$633	$795	$638	$710
372	661	815	663	679	425	843	1168	936	1168
373	691	846	714	754	426	819	894	700	913
374	585	699	598	602	427	767	951	807	869
375	777	933	771	794	429	631	796	655	777
376	598	767	651	672	430	810	1003	824	922
377	758	922	727	746	431	622	733	589	717
378	664	823	609	626	432	755	902	683	857
379	623	766	587	629	433	725	915	689	854
380	461	536	470	471	434	708	891	653	781
381	381	483	424	427	435	707	902	692	785
382	461	501	466	466	436	701	950	696	790
383	406	456	493	499	437	593	749	557	626
384	796	1056	846	992	438	639	782	557	613
385	809	1152	976	1063	439	271	702	389	451
386	652	939	772	873	440	606	873	589	681
387	673	896	796	877	441	536	712	660	689
388	544	752	699	737	442	797	1006	841	984
389	773	924	774	833	444	547	679	542	619
390	701	881	649	709	445	816	1033	819	957
391	743	958	725	758	446	653	841	747	865
392	553	752	570	633	447	852	1055	939	1027
393	715	963	708	771	448	622	833	716	782
394	553	749	471	514	449	827	1073	977	1116
395	619	822	519	541	451	749	992	853	994
396	507	736	486	541	452	757	902	763	905
397	1023	1267	1065	1232	453	822	973	781	958
398	829	1127	917	1062	454	731	994	763	995
399	541	769	639	769	455	514	702	582	746
400	779	1073	880	1015	456	518	687	600	719
401	773	1037	864	983	457	526	615	606	734
402	799	1014	808	921	458	496	561	527	638
404	716	1028	704	743	459	681	854	734	840
405	671	878	578	617	460	740	938	772	887
406	702	976	614	661	461	824	995	878	996
407	657	937	585	667	462	452	638	575	709
408	464	653	468	559	463	898	1030	989	1104
410	984	1357	1214	1712	464	723	848	798	887
411	1173	1552	1142	1297	465	644	744	685	814
412	1146	1461	1038	1198	466	603	571	490	566
413	947	1229	1026	1248	467	632	673	624	811
420	1015	1454	1274	1949	468	855	938	875	1019
422	1141	1400	989	1124	469	807	1092	1095	1538

(2) The Central Core (Grand Street, North to 14th Street)

Blocks	*1905*	*1913*	*1921*	*1929*	*Blocks*	*1905*	*1913*	*1921*	*1929*
470	1093	1322	1166	1215	485	1349	1013	669	670
471	925	1071	944	951	486	1198	918	646	646
473	2403	1999	1380	1412	487	1028	866	631	635
474	3268	2296	1573	1573	488	601	618	524	540
475	1677	1332	929	1938	489	611	657	566	591
483	2551	2009	1361	1361	492	786	866	783	883
484	2830	2087	1516	1475	493	268	463	410	256

Blocks	1905	1913	1921	1929
494	$ 562	$ 642	$ 565	$ 601
495	633	704	655	704
497	2566	1962	1400	1411
498	2908	2132	1536	1536
499	1323	997	661	661
500	1167	899	604	607
501	974	811	544	565
502	653	661	536	555
503	649	691	625	645
507	855	892	856	1010
508	650	733	693	707
509	307	332	324	339
512	2982	2143	1612	1577
513	1350	1029	643	656
514	1244	945	632	632
515	1042	895	619	662
516	675	691	581	601
517	559	603	550	562
518	605	690	593	692
521	1208	1296	1170	1255
523	3606	2634	1876	1879
524	1877	1556	1032	1048
525	1168	1247	1008	1031
531	2265	2224	1565	1565
532	2952	2298	1590	1590
533	1379	1097	607	607
534	1218	1014	589	633
535	2361	2000	1295	1310
536	1037	906	566	597
537	695	697	555	555
538	804	798	604	790
539	628	672	580	596
540	635	673	591	636
543	836	836	669	1176
544	2638	2102	1645	1649
545	5731	5232	3486	3486
546	2721	2292	1376	1482
547	2358	2130	1186	1204
548	4324	3952	1035	1189
550	1402	1467	1020	2104
551	1496	1499	1116	2202
552	1271	1296	1172	1973
553	816	817	665	1158
555	2098	2328	1755	1792
556	1229	1328	1187	1319
557	1822	1791	1163	1163
558	910	1042	912	980

Blocks	1905	1913	1921	1929
559	$1851	$2600	$2415	$3295
560	2556	2527	1682	1795
561	2435	2384	1391	1470
562	2660	2462	1460	1597
563	2307	2203	1281	1440
564	3505	3375	2000	2019
565	3960	4064	3247	4337
566	1147	1191	793	1524
567	1127	1217	880	1743
568	1309	1368	906	1778
569	1427	1487	980	1727
570	1494	1530	1074	1627
571	2971	3044	2217	3637
572	1853	1918	1724	2961
574	1620	1631	1438	2549
575	1539	1523	1303	2252
576	2189	2242	1817	2756
577	5383	5468	4056	6086
578	734	747	859	1567
579	973	1015	1021	1724
580	934	1013	1107	1855
581	788	804	935	2653
584	542	564	538	730
585	443	399	442	661
588	860	878	775	1250
589	527	576	492	740
590	876	922	818	1128
593	593	633	541	858
607	723	779	789	1027
608	1244	1275	1286	1803
609	1634	1672	1425	2064
614	593	612	722	1060
615	888	941	921	1237
616	493	508	452	646
617	631	632	654	1009
618	907	981	984	1890
619	910	943	889	1221
620	889	875	833	1124
621	756	798	747	960
622	646	674	660	894
623	590	614	588	771
624	727	743	685	864
625	526	561	507	651
626	581	615	572	667
627	550	575	592	699
628	293	309	309	355
629	896	992	964	1587

(3) West of Hudson Street (Grand Street, North to 14th Street)

Blocks	1905	1913	1921	1929
594	933	1048	1046	1541
595	875	1040	996	1339
596	975	1107	1066	1345
597	808	922	921	1225
598	870	1367	924	1193
599	863	990	922	1166

Blocks	1905	1913	1921	1929	Blocks	1905	1913	1921	1929
600.......	$866	$1361	$963	$1329	636.......	$762	$794	$779	$925
601.......	870	963	953	1202	637.......	775	818	803	896
602.......	839	970	921	1160	638.......	407	429	411	462
604.......	316	372	342	463	639.......	547	605	640	710
631.......	540	555	501	571	640.......	673	700	681	774
632.......	523	546	479	559	641.......	650	689	653	738
633.......	550	567	501	568	642.......	607	628	629	702
634.......	540	583	540	623	643.......	744	814	772	929
635.......	338	354	344	400	646.......	840	1005	1450	1860

D. From 14th Street, North to 25th Street

(1) West of Ninth Avenue to Hudson River

Blocks	1905	1913	1921	1929	Blocks	1905	1913	1921	1929
669.......	551	800	753	859	715.......	642	663	752	889
670.......	343	521	574	717	716.......	657	694	764	897
694.......	852	1087	1244	1447	717.......	649	738	760	903
695.......	806	1001	1084	1294	719.......	706	758	811	1193
696.......	532	693	831	1075	720.......	872	884	991	1602
712.......	864	1084	1547	1890	721.......	814	821	899	1223
713.......	752	799	908	1110	722.......	680	705	733	1024
714.......	642	661	763	937					

(2) Central Core (14th Street, North to 25th Street)

Blocks	1905	1913	1921	1929	Blocks	1905	1913	1921	1929
738.......	929	1021	1140	2064	798.......	4099	4240	3007	3469
739.......	745	769	858	1388	799.......	2855	3446	3003	3419
740.......	681	699	769	1150	800.......	1606	2985	2925	3142
741.......	773	796	840	1282	816.......	4830	5363	3897	4041
742.......	714	727	761	968	817.......	2426	2415	1774	1796
743.......	765	768	820	1241	818.......	3759	4062	2911	2915
744.......	686	714	781	1164	819.......	3977	4685	3314	3379
745.......	835	916	991	1538	820.......	5111	5321	3745	3761
746.......	1042	1084	1099	2170	821.......	4044	4618	3066	3066
747.......	1243	1259	1223	2236	822.......	4429	4732	3199	3192
748.......	817	866	941	1501	823.......	5835	5886	3669	3709
764.......	943	964	1098	2200	824.......	15107	12408	5488	5704
765.......	706	781	863	1464	825.......	8014	7915	6806	6815
766.......	739	835	925	1504	826.......	4917	6123	5809	4459
767.......	784	888	1021	1696	842.......	3280	3816	2484	2496
768.......	808	873	1036	1702	843.......	3036	3327	2204	2363
769.......	784	880	998	1634	844.......	3105	3337	2261	2248
770.......	871	971	1035	1731	846.......	5714	6392	4733	4667
771.......	1003	1092	1196	2059	847.......	6014	7132	5047	4959
772.......	1713	1752	1597	2886	848.......	5778	6765	4733	4603
773.......	1352	1574	1617	2671	849.......	5588	6914	4962	4879
774.......	865	1074	1356	1995	850.......	5732	7141	5213	5210
790.......	1646	1719	1410	1975	851.......	6506	9327	7226	7829
791.......	1598	1604	1559	1976	853.......	2876	4240	4680	4880
792.......	1570	1625	1479	1840	854.......	1893	2907	3014	3196
793.......	1872	1841	1664	1867	870.......	2276	3126	3605	5585
794.......	2732	2641	1788	1992	871.......	1803	2865	2792	2957
795.......	2674	2759	1784	1984	872.......	1417	2229	2075	2256
796.......	2389	2658	1692	1980	873.......	1594	2734	2769	3277
797.......	2745	3145	1927	2257	874.......	1573	2640	2816	3291

Blocks	1905	1913	1921	1929	Blocks	1905	1913	1921	1929
875	$1473	$2251	$2408	$3064	878	$1393	$2484	$2620	$2935
876	941	1609	1661	1936	879	2096	3641	3636	4188
877	1372	2220	2160	2775	880	1515	2482	2846	3245

(3) East of Third Avenue (14th Street, North to 25th Street)

Blocks	1905	1913	1921	1929	Blocks	1905	1913	1921	1929
896	867	1082	1040	1652	947	514	668	625	726
897	629	710	718	1053	948	359	523	484	563
898	546	686	675	908	949	386	605	519	608
899	661	810	768	1248	950	366	555	455	532
900	502	675	596	938	951	251	489	418	515
901	505	653	583	928	952	412	523	479	559
902	544	692	643	998	953	500	560	550	620
903	781	1077	941	1394	954	471	680	567	644
904	453	572	536	720	955	449	671	554	631
905	641	790	769	1123	956	281	415	365	437
921	697	788	708	1003	972	452	640	523	624
922	533	582	528	720	973	457	560	509	589
923	635	647	653	1039	974	359	449	426	503
924	653	694	680	1040	975	329	435	416	487
925	312	356	323	436	976	361	470	462	553
926	406	460	423	535	978	360	421	438	551
927	582	730	690	937	982	431	554	518	625
928	643	803	742	976	983	376	469	426	524
929	602	729	630	758	984	345	447	385	478
930	545	663	599	764	985	335	432	413	519
946	598	763	683	887					

II. The Midtown District

A. From 25th to 40th Streets

(1) West of Ninth Avenue

Blocks	1905	1913	1921	1929	Blocks	1905	1913	1921	1929
671	370	520	590	795	708	535	618	803	1064
672	400	525	650	870	709	456	547	734	977
673	425	560	710	940	710	505	629	788	1123
674	440	549	710	938	711	527	694	793	1211
675	477	555	771	949	723	669	703	803	953
685	522	667	842	1045	724	636	712	798	977
698	534	690	813	1082	726	611	660	768	991
699	494	598	732	924	728	646	653	800	1094
700	500	583	754	911	731	561	777	779	1485
701	528	611	762	905	732	653	814	859	1422
702	420	552	652	882	733	659	747	797	1394
703	471	612	702	892	734	619	703	777	1312
705	706	877	1076	1704	735	689	794	846	1472
706	687	818	1034	1327	736	601	720	765	1312
707	484	517	761	980	737	652	785	818	1467

(2) Central Core (25th to 40th Streets)

Blocks	1905	1913	1921	1929	Blocks	1905	1913	1921	1929
749	716	732	782	1283	753	901	1090	1048	2115
750	859	898	926	1567	754	976	1293	1273	2635
751	776	853	844	1518	757	1388	1999	2186	3998
752	866	992	984	1796	758	1344	1667	1769	5343

Blocks	1905	1913	1921	1929
759	$ 753	$1009	$1038	$3516
760	882	1222	1308	4254
761	918	1580	1327	4252
762	915	1320	1331	4277
763	925	1365	1359	4005
775	1019	1238	1567	2504
776	968	1289	1645	3093
777	1002	1329	1730	3324
778	1026	1447	1843	4057
779	1080	1624	2010	4950
780	1194	1680	1845	4165
783	2999	4105	4495	9140
784	2429	3726	3358	9109
785	1224	2656	2763	8315
786	1265	2888	2918	8484
787	1323	3022	2963	8677
788	1318	3062	2970	8458
789	1423	3075	3080	8534
801	1485	3057	3190	3657
802	1557	3261	3265	3823
803	1464	2922	3044	3768
804	1571	2931	3408	4551
805	1476	2987	3027	4205
806	2094	4399	3750	6476
809	5272	8847	10877	14565
810	5189	7036	7952	12314
811	5092	6333	8108	11140
812	5198	6525	7492	11420
813	4728	6473	8058	12358
814	4875	6316	7788	11778
815	5293	6515	8160	12861
827	6606	7326	6336	5860
828	5984	8726	6895	7298
829	6552	9560	6486	7109
830	7019	9836	6671	7799
831	6093	9149	5873	7041
832	7503	10801	7621	8639
833	7594	12483	9736	11181

Blocks	1905	1913	1921	1929
834	6828	11169	10283	11879
835	9720	21750	18457	24062
836	8200	19679	19433	25774
837	5016	9391	9407	13461
838	4718	8936	9317	13956
839	3921	7449	7415	11337
840	4931	8919	10611	14781
841	5113	9411	11000	16096
855	1586	2441	2623	2762
856	5145	7873	6794	7215
857	3959	6579	5438	6447
858	3637	6187	5162	6363
859	3622	6215	5367	6320
860	3934	6412	5967	6913
861	4324	7216	6551	7623
862	4188	7507	5874	9136
863	4885	11328	10273	13695
864	5186	11336	12310	16245
865	4923	7607	7846	11922
866	5006	8592	8943	13195
867	5387	8237	9207	13533
868	5295	8161	8614	12892
869	5192	8351	9521	16033
881	924	1670	1917	2153
882	1428	2368	2581	3027
883	1398	2356	2598	3031
884	1187	1898	2234	2646
885	1319	2125	2330	2791
886	1353	2241	2568	3035
887	1400	2296	2596	3378
888	546	2448	2938	3965
889	661	1953	1780	2786
890	1951	3380	3029	4777
891	1914	2814	2756	4318
892	2029	2952	2883	4466
893	2050	2756	2724	4432
894	2134	2873	2769	4745
895	1864	2685	2515	4547

(3) East of Third Avenue (25th to 40th Streets)

Blocks	1905	1913	1921	1929
906	627	740	724	1054
907	627	722	701	1045
908	494	565	551	832
909	618	716	702	1165
910	614	719	712	1079
911	516	619	649	964
912	569	681	665	955
913	537	652	626	878
914	781	991	817	1508
915	761	935	798	1781
916	635	708	680	1547
917	587	656	653	1456
918	479	546	529	1231
919	635	714	677	1656

Blocks	1905	1913	1921	1929
920	597	668	654	1594
931	454	533	518	670
932	544	619	606	773
933	454	500	502	639
934	460	520	514	634
935	503	623	601	760
936	523	611	602	800
937	473	590	549	816
940	428	598	517	1038
942	396	517	447	977
943	488	624	533	1256
944	475	593	483	1270
945	483	598	490	1262
957	223	357	241	302

B. *From 40th to 59th Streets*

(1) West of Ninth Avenue

Blocks	*1905*	*1913*	*1921*	*1929*	*Blocks*	*1905*	*1913*	*1921*	*1929*
1050......	637	831	895	1646	1073......	442	584	754	1145
1051......	752	1036	1237	2378	1074......	511	671	870	1297
1052......	824	1127	1416	2428	1075......	511	681	939	1331
1053......	675	857	1065	1596	1076......	526	674	863	1305
1054......	681	840	1035	1552	1077......	493	632	820	1231
1055......	718	871	1025	1545	1078......	499	659	850	1276
1056......	712	835	984	1518	1079......	455	588	768	1121
1057......	732	879	1060	1535	1080......	519	664	763	1285
1058......	753	907	1049	1503	1081......	483	618	745	1112
1059......	571	704	826	1246	1082......	529	705	861	1334
1060......	680	847	991	1482	1083......	448	628	775	1135
1061......	541	699	781	1205	1084......	460	658	906	1364
1062......	672	859	958	1470	1085......	500	724	1003	1463
1063......	651	822	955	1527	1086......	539	722	975	1501
1064......	572	750	959	1554	1087......	340	502	575	925
1065......	608	773	1018	1658	1088......	483	625	879	1077
1066......	778	895	1091	1937	1089......	525	800	1050	1400
1067......	691	807	1004	1788	1099......	433	643	850	1059
1069......	444	616	753	1104	1102......	427	427	302	1200
1070......	609	868	1103	1646	1104......	318	456	723	1177
1071......	591	838	1072	1627	1105......	381	559	861	1256
1072......	501	669	870	1312	1106......	450	600	860	1180

(2) Central Core (40th to 59th Streets)

Blocks	1905	1913	1921	1929	Blocks	1905	1913	1921	1929
993......	5137	6936	9659	14550	1019......	2645	4516	6541	9628
994......	6901	10725	15962	22475	1020......	2309	4079	5905	9131
996......	3343	6287	8471	12463	1021......	2246	3960	5715	9014
997......	3400	5548	7702	11524	1022......	2324	3566	5245	8718
998......	2580	4593	6625	10092	1023......	2442	3335	4888	7853
999......	2179	3993	5578	8938	1024......	1758	2555	3944	6513
1000......	2418	3978	5684	8893	1025......	1859	2537	3739	5733
1001......	2097	3190	4666	7590	1026......	2318	3248	4945	7697
1002......	1763	2561	3440	6616	1027......	2592	3459	5205	8743
1003......	1600	2610	3500	7350	1028......	2656	4068	6066	10020
1004......	1727	2344	2799	5471	1029......	2825	4419	6488	9877
1005......	6485	2090	2510	4618	1030......	2811	4392	6703	9870
1006......	1480	2031	2562	4935	1031......	929	1478	1773	4102
1007......	1664	2138	2844	5338	1032......	1260	1846	2423	5730
1008......	2043	2466	3385	6608	1033......	1053	1581	2075	4482
1009......	2483	3243	4619	10554	1034......	1003	1518	1919	3701
1010......	2259	2993	4389	9788	1035......	1050	1458	1796	3758
1011......	3131	4248	6370	10315	1036......	1005	1342	1722	3415
1012......	1327	2604	3184	7929	1037......	1033	1415	1712	3149
1013......	2939	5179	8369	13975	1038......	841	1153	1362	2512
1014......	3216	5926	8891	14178	1039......	954	1284	1534	3004
1015......	2515	4681	6778	11498	1040......	1040	1377	1711	3611
1016......	2797	4365	6700	10922	1041......	950	1207	1416	2781
1017......	2383	3804	5651	9241	1042......	1099	1365	1592	3063
1018......	1951	3436	4892	7833	1043......	865	1108	1274	2572

Blocks	*1905*	*1913*	*1921*	*1929*	*Blocks*	*1905*	*1913*	*1921*	*1929*
1044......	$ 763	$1042	$1342	$2684	1285......	$5330	$7174	$8534	$17256
1045......	877	1214	1533	3017	1286......	2019	2169	2573	4899
1046......	1143	1521	1816	3525	1287......	4812	5710	6899	12293
1047......	1116	1622	2358	4943	1288......	5281	6364	7437	14578
1048......	1425	2135	2906	6188	1289......	5380	6186	7130	14728
1049......	1809	2420	3294	4800	1290......	5015	5825	6965	14638
1258......	7731	12755	16930	31350	1291......	5355	6085	7154	15623
1259......	5572	9088	10476	16474	1292......	6447	7588	9188	20285
1260......	5571	9125	10522	15715	1293......	5917	6616	7963	16729
1261......	4163	8564	9758	14075	1294......	5812	6600	7450	16500
1262......	5559	7909	8565	13479	1295......	1731	4004	3462	8111
1263......	5594	7406	7986	13910	1301......	1162	1864	3141	8451
1264......	5567	5346	5435	9042	1303......	1148	1826	3201	7834
1265......	5495	6855	7165	11666	1304......	857	1504	2638	7327
1266......	5802	6961	7557	11377	1305......	805	939	1279	3967
1267......	6358	7413	7992	11580	1306......	880	1229	2115	5545
1268......	6474	7404	7421	11300	1307......	831	1274	2019	5151
1269......	4979	5611	5449	8412	1308......	1035	1550	2275	5944
1270......	6196	7106	7753	12288	1309......	1120	1540	2194	5547
1271......	4727	5147	5661	9050	1310......	1320	1678	2223	5775
1272......	7496	8338	11150	19131	1311......	1543	2019	2647	8507
1273......	8154	8596	10764	18185	1312......	1709	2061	2622	9208
1275......	5016	8304	10934	21675	1313......	1872	2213	2749	9996

(3) East of Third Avenue (40th to 59th Streets)

Blocks	*1905*	*1913*	*1921*	*1929*	*Blocks*	*1905*	*1913*	*1921*	*1929*
1314......	598	687	683	1856	1336......	463	565	569	1788
1315......	618	701	713	2814	1337......	476	571	571	1277
1316......	701	765	745	3886	1338......	480	577	576	1189
1317......	617	667	662	2258	1339......	412	501	499	1060
1318......	567	592	605	1981	1341......	472	577	576	1208
1320......	558	572	568	1470	1342......	470	545	517	1354
1321......	607	634	651	1737	1343......	476	558	508	1358
1322......	571	601	643	1750	1344......	434	530	476	1209
1323......	483	596	587	1533	1345......	501	594	552	1337
1324......	605	613	611	1495	1346......	483	583	522	1254
1325......	597	599	598	1345	1347......	447	677	529	1326
1326......	602	632	606	1353	1348......	347	478	433	1106
1327......	601	670	634	1407	1349......	497	649	605	2851
1328......	638	686	646	1436	1350......	527	708	662	3130
1329......	621	657	619	1512	1351......	531	759	686	1563
1330......	558	613	593	1799	1365......	320	410	408	893
1331......	629	695	707	2352	1366......	317	411	413	932
1332......	737	883	884	2410	1367......	324	428	417	1188
1333......	430	503	468	1904	1368......	366	433	444	3405
1334......	452	550	528	2712	1369......	387	512	511	3116
1335......	345	429	420	1817	1370......	310	386	359	1244

III. The Central Park Area (59th to 96th Streets)

A. West of Central Park

Blocks	*1905*	*1913*	*1921*	*1929*	*Blocks*	*1905*	*1913*	*1921*	*1929*
1112......	1603	2517	3107	4495	1114......	1885	3325	4298	6445
1113......	2250	3962	5008	6909	1115......	2080	3589	4570	6557

Blocks	1905	1913	1921	1929
1116......	$ 992	$1669	$2161	$3224
1117......	1419	2276	2945	4678
1118......	1105	1519	2167	3533
1119......	1323	1763	2606	4143
1120......	1095	1388	1931	3130
1121......	1516	1716	2322	3769
1122......	1461	1502	2174	3328
1123......	1613	1751	2447	3808
1124......	2456	2693	3402	5565
1125......	2553	2784	3678	5815
1126......	1798	1947	2760	4123
1127......	1749	1909	2640	4024
1128......	1567	1612	2188	3328
1129......	1665	1842	2357	3641
1132......	758	832	1049	1482
1133......	388	455	553	768
1134......	856	1066	1333	2024
1135......	834	1122	1447	2260
1136......	1100	1551	2016	3195
1137......	890	1409	1728	2423
1138......	1405	2318	2977	4151
1139......	684	992	1305	2083
1140......	1394	1903	2639	3888
1141......	1638	2145	2969	4195
1142......	1076	1245	1743	3594
1143......	2012	2939	3981	6765
1144......	2108	2643	3622	6478
1145......	1261	1453	2207	3538
1146......	1301	1491	1989	3131
1147......	1211	1365	1805	2895
1148......	1222	1423	1841	3056
1149......	1161	1219	1591	2534
1150......	1242	1451	2088	3779
1151......	435	466	641	961
1152......	428	503	732	1089
1153......	441	509	746	1119
1154......	402	494	771	1030
1155......	431	584	904	1187
1156......	419	623	881	1205
1157......	500	675	950	1315
1158......	430	642	826	1118
1160......	481	683	1024	1284
1161......	770	1032	1638	2169
1162......	1295	1713	2467	3320
1163......	1799	1995	2962	5164
1164......	1474	2137	3191	4894
1165......	1671	2619	3793	5407
1166......	1532	2367	3212	5295
1167......	1546	2300	3233	4548
1168......	1301	2019	2758	3823
1169......	1143	1702	2500	3462
1170......	1451	2271	3450	4598
1171......	371	455	557	761

Blocks	1905	1913	1921	1929
1184......	$2469	$3300	$4778	$6054
1185......	1769	2285	3123	3875
1186......	1431	1922	2743	3557
1195......	1908	2070	2212	4681
1196......	1304	1500	1650	2984
1197......	1217	1392	1481	2841
1198......	1264	1435	1533	2717
1199......	1564	1947	2116	3792
1200......	1542	1704	1964	3968
1201......	1318	1430	1626	2827
1202......	1323	1441	1651	2742
1203......	1325	1442	1545	2718
1204......	1334	1462	1480	2632
1205......	1268	1415	1544	2557
1206......	1244	1367	1410	2451
1207......	1149	1384	1414	2463
1208......	1109	1308	1318	2405
1209......	1071	1148	1176	2746
1210......	1307	1513	1975	3649
1211......	1150	1305	1581	2567
1212......	1143	1258	1459	2545
1213......	1051	1198	1432	2351
1214......	1074	1217	1442	2323
1215......	1036	1199	1384	2314
1216......	1224	1428	1784	3479
1217......	1048	1321	1784	3050
1218......	969	1302	1448	2378
1219......	808	956	1136	1953
1220......	833	954	1233	2007
1221......	942	1067	1316	1980
1222......	559	632	722	1220
1223......	766	832	947	1435
1224......	997	1105	1276	2125
1225......	916	1024	1162	2023
1226......	943	1137	1242	2348
1227......	1148	1915	2528	3554
1228......	1044	1695	2299	3099
1229......	1161	1944	2619	3631
1231......	1124	1873	2518	3585
1232......	1142	1849	2530	3638
1233......	1393	2238	3060	4477
1234......	1071	1904	2724	3975
1235......	1201	1962	2605	3835
1236......	982	1522	2362	3471
1237......	1150	1946	2825	4025
1239......	1133	1825	2439	3498
1241......	834	1260	1764	2732
1242......	1085	1614	2289	3416
1243......	1114	1736	2468	3546
1244......	1811	2429	2968	4396
1245......	1626	2196	2725	3868
1246......	1019	1385	1657	2356
1247......	1085	1702	2222	3128

Blocks	1905	1913	1921	1929
1248......	$1023	$1398	$1821	$2883
1249......	1044	1383	1763	2548
1250......	1941	2526	3018	4731
1251......	$1288	$1794	$2153	$3039
1252......	1340	2098	2424	2602
1253......	1255	2069	2243	2746

B. East of Central Park

Blocks	1905	1913	1921	1929
1374......	6509	6876	7188	14653
1375......	5657	6000	5997	9397
1376......	5545	5884	6011	8615
1377......	5261	5697	5788	8440
1378......	5381	5874	5675	8253
1379......	5520	6011	5542	7971
1380......	3861	4240	4151	6007
1381......	5906	6281	5952	8020
1382......	6139	6415	6089	7852
1383......	6193	6586	6356	9075
1384......	5928	6265	6244	8183
1385......	4010	4658	4426	9090
1386......	5396	5635	5449	8076
1387......	5770	5634	5485	7916
1388......	4636	4714	4627	5975
1389......	4940	5157	4892	6760
1390......	3873	4071	4109	5817
1391......	4438	4670	4716	6604
1392......	4592	4787	4833	6878
1393......	5319	5598	5431	7959
1394......	2261	2449	3149	8566
1395......	1965	2287	2765	5723
1396......	1833	2276	2682	5075
1397......	1643	1888	2502	5250
1398......	1253	1487	1994	3810
1399......	1604	1930	2207	4472
1400......	1172	1445	1713	3173
1401......	661	795	922	1750
1402......	676	740	1145	2178
1404......	2033	2204	2689	4680
1405......	1800	2133	2522	4569
1406......	2034	2359	2680	5698
1407......	1972	2149	2315	5953
1408......	1429	1862	2153	4107
1409......	1257	1435	1870	3875
1410......	1077	1267	1643	3298
1411......	431	441	595	1024
1412......	1122	1403	1847	3853
1413......	1574	1704	2292	5059
1414......	738	934	924	2041
1415......	722	817	776	1361
1416......	625	750	711	1221
1417......	522	601	564	894
1418......	380	408	398	601
1419......	562	659	657	982
1420......	650	750	850	1100
1421......	625	726	744	1124
1422......	591	681	686	1250
1423......	584	670	672	1135
1424......	585	672	657	1171
1425......	408	458	459	741
1426......	617	625	647	1422
1427......	599	649	608	1421
1428......	574	650	584	1058
1429......	568	648	606	1026
1430......	455	519	496	803
1431......	609	609	588	954
1432......	537	655	617	1048
1433......	564	627	642	1292
1435......	412	593	536	696
1436......	374	486	491	662
1437......	378	494	487	648
1438......	348	551	543	743
1439......	432	586	585	816
1440......	400	559	566	802
1441......	405	587	654	864
1443......	376	537	553	600
1444......	410	550	574	534
1445......	353	496	507	790
1446......	425	560	596	1654
1447......	440	598	614	1428
1448......	403	565	584	857
1449......	385	552	559	820
1450......	405	580	588	874
1451......	407	571	584	858
1452......	385	585	584	424
1453......	433	586	599	1681
1455......	290	355	377	580
1456......	251	362	395	535
1457......	299	416	433	579
1458......	179	245	269	365
1459......	339	482	560	790
1460......	300	437	487	753
1461......	139	232	234	371
1462......	134	181	205	357
1463......	215	334	358	619
1464......	304	440	472	768
1465......	305	438	476	763
1466......	318	467	490	425
1467......	324	485	511	1517
1468......	288	429	462	795
1469......	307	443	483	768

Blocks	1905	1913	1921	1929
1470	$ 299	$ 443	$ 467	$1175
1471	305	453	495	793
1472	294	426	468	778
1473	358	504	542	1153
1482	199	311	336	584
1483	251	365	391	814
1484	241	386	398	804
1485	203	298	304	476
1486	351	438	503	642
1487	220	316	334	557
1490	341	579	586	1314
1491	4391	4844	5201	7356
1492	3763	4126	4305	5977
1493	2805	3306	3572	4725
1494	3422	4064	4212	5336
1495	2615	2840	3083	3465
1497	2250	2977	3667	5129
1498	2919	3245	3711	5934
1499	2945	3236	3400	9257
1500	2999	3155	3247	5790
1501	2135	2225	2251	4514
1502	3351	3480	3647	5860
1503	3042	3119	3429	5475
1504	2783	2889	3026	5546
1505	2691	2759	2954	3049
1506	1924	1613	1967	3866
1507	2277	2097	2203	3502
1508	1312	1589	2382	5840
1509	1115	1506	2073	5740
1510	1031	1368	1811	3723
1511	1006	1365	1731	3244
1512	997	1401	1778	2715
1513	1032	1400	1711	5216
1514	990	1241	2238	5118
1515	996	1375	2260	5403
1516	732	985	1231	2906
1517	934	1204	1403	3379
1518	962	1226	1417	3470
1519	878	1163	1339	3227
1520	839	1096	1259	2936
1521	881	1127	1228	3261
1522	938	1144	1335	3358
1523	866	1101	1132	2227
1524	800	968	962	2310
1525	523	587	617	1730
1526	541	649	644	1045
1527	575	672	671	1050
1528	574	688	684	1046
1529	532	628	625	1004
1530	570	707	697	1074
1531	693	777	836	1252
1532	666	782	822	2120

Blocks	1905	1913	1921	1929
1533	$ 553	$ 704	$ 598	$1121
1534	507	645	645	846
1535	468	566	567	883
1536	492	591	566	940
1537	470	530	510	749
1538	491	557	520	548
1539	460	537	489	995
1540	435	532	455	769
1541	483	576	495	1227
1542	502	595	618	1294
1543	470	560	578	1015
1544	442	550	567	925
1545	406	508	525	817
1546	440	561	576	928
1547	414	547	559	878
1548	459	607	625	1240
1549	463	607	619	1199
1550	314	453	472	705
1551	356	566	569	875
1552	346	559	575	799
1553	335	556	554	761
1554	247	422	396	581
1555	308	530	476	701
1556	304	530	463	660
1557	286	538	450	647
1558	267	414	348	505
1559	321	409	438	1016
1560	372	495	515	973
1561	357	482	508	980
1562	348	491	510	955
1563	347	487	508	939
1564	343	494	514	936
1565	283	403	403	1045
1566	306	415	430	1058
1567	326	433	475	852
1568	249	403	393	717
1569	310	466	440	821
1570	255	483	425	648
1571	237	484	407	573
1572	224	428	416	542
1573	246	361	286	449
1576	325	487	461	1772
1577	271	403	384	1121
1578	218	346	342	978
1579	301	459	459	1244
1580	319	472	472	1321
1581	323	475	475	1550
1582	343	501	503	2145
1583	237	360	350	1192
1584	310	463	464	1108
1585	310	466	444	1822

IV. North of 96th Street

A. East of Lenox Avenue

Blocks	1905	1913	1921	1929
1595......	$ 709	$1022	$1025	$1203
1596......	774	1172	1121	1329
1597......	693	1062	956	1283
1598......	803	1138	1096	1347
1599......	874	1332	1358	2758
1600......	758	1147	1159	1741
1601......	855	1193	1120	1307
1602......	1675	1653	1828	3805
1603......	1320	1253	1324	2309
1604......	839	823	839	1495
1605......	846	627	593	931
1606......	336	409	388	540
1607......	991	967	965	1715
1608......	784	875	868	1408
1609......	417	569	516	723
1611......	742	905	714	977
1612......	970	1073	1057	1540
1613......	764	915	811	1147
1614......	757	877	825	1117
1615......	789	956	906	1265
1616......	760	976	901	1223
1617......	725	946	930	1290
1618......	681	971	940	1269
1619......	662	939	935	1320
1620......	706	986	951	1431
1621......	833	1157	1071	1740
1622......	792	1174	1137	1635
1623......	709	1023	901	1151
1624......	635	840	791	1481
1625......	542	792	731	958
1626......	615	810	875	1030
1627......	546	787	789	962
1628......	480	736	669	883
1629......	485	731	695	849
1630......	451	740	723	904
1631......	489	784	721	932
1632......	549	675	606	761
1633......	471	674	595	847
1634......	600	866	792	1081
1635......	572	834	714	1006
1636......	572	841	677	964
1637......	534	849	755	995
1638......	563	855	741	1054
1639......	417	595	538	674
1640......	577	865	785	979
1641......	518	783	721	923
1642......	530	771	653	867
1643......	802	1012	967	1629
1644......	750	1016	957	1587
1645......	539	797	733	951
1646......	$401	$552	$472	$603
1647......	323	519	408	527
1648......	304	512	433	563
1649......	256	419	343	457
1650......	244	405	336	429
1651......	321	557	468	589
1652......	276	489	387	452
1653......	339	539	448	585
1654......	322	441	357	498
1655......	369	551	460	661
1656......	399	598	500	649
1657......	362	524	427	527
1658......	366	503	432	534
1659......	297	407	341	424
1660......	356	485	444	557
1661......	360	488	435	555
1662......	327	434	386	486
1663......	380	515	463	560
1664......	400	552	467	573
1665......	432	637	539	775
1666......	525	681	585	844
1667......	743	588	545	640
1668......	380	525	590	600
1669......	290	357	290	420
1670......	290	525	630	543
1671......	282	396	351	532
1672......	301	424	416	590
1673......	312	448	403	603
1674......	311	463	411	576
1675......	300	430	380	529
1676......	267	378	324	456
1677......	345	497	424	581
1678......	350	502	433	587
1679......	305	431	390	552
1680......	247	373	316	476
1681......	293	408	359	490
1682......	329	506	576	576
1683......	293	467	405	505
1684......	322	519	442	552
1685......	288	445	381	481
1686......	319	526	474	593
1687......	352	558	519	682
1689......	320	475	434	830
1697......	270	453	389	549
1698......	296	545	465	601
1699......	381	585	491	588
1700......	379	497	413	530
1704......	285	450	484	495
1708......	246	446	409	448
1709......	270	402	383	447

Blocks	*1905*	*1913*	*1921*	*1929*
1710	$ 289	$ 460	$ 435	$ 524
1711	260	418	376	422
1717	835	1144	878	1299
1718	890	1178	857	1244
1720	863	1064	815	1082
1721	978	1249	973	1261
1722	2102	3022	2177	3205
1723	1551	2167	2010	2845
1724	809	1022	686	1110
1725	831	1066	648	1018
1726	764	987	602	927
1727	815	922	617	1027
1728	740	823	512	917
1729	684	784	506	924
1730	618	747	511	883
1731	618	795	535	931
1732	616	906	711	1117
1733	630	1037	707	1115
1734	255	413	261	429
1735	459	727	449	806
1736	378	457	287	482
1737	377	638	413	644
1745	761	970	745	1084
1746	745	920	686	954
1747	797	868	671	951
1748	550	915	510	752
1749	1490	2018	1360	2096
1750	1353	1750	1420	2012
1751	765	883	568	762
1752	577	682	442	573
1753	657	823	515	667
1754	575	632	403	529
1755	607	677	437	566
1756	595	652	441	575
1757	503	572	369	522
1758	436	542	395	509
1759	456	569	452	556

Blocks	*1905*	*1913*	*1921*	*1929*
1767	$ 597	$ 983	$ 872	$1182
1768	657	968	890	1106
1769	712	905	843	1121
1770	717	992	927	1185
1771	675	1006	961	1212
1772	689	1027	961	1199
1773	1703	2047	2116	2896
1774	1553	1820	1757	2373
1775	624	751	586	699
1776	598	719	520	682
1777	620	846	566	670
1778	596	714	816	851
1783	455	659	569	735
1784	400	545	495	667
1785	472	690	643	812
1786	468	717	666	917
1787	474	697	641	838
1788	471	693	673	896
1789	654	838	817	1152
1790	499	561	476	630
1791	456	528	410	419
1792	433	494	353	352
1795	319	437	403	496
1796	318	453	420	510
1797	325	465	415	512
1798	324	462	424	513
1799	310	457	398	498
1800	317	467	428	510
1801	383	560	480	577
1806	232	352	310	357
1807	237	349	308	366
1808	178	282	256	295
1809	237	356	328	400
1810	247	336	296	372
1811	259	327	266	359
1812	298	447	409	500

B. West of Lenox Avenue

Blocks	*1905*	*1913*	*1921*	*1929*	*Blocks*	*1905*	*1913*	*1921*	*1929*
1820	795	1066	1053	1327	1833	880	1218	1054	1726
1821	734	989	1014	1166	1834	848	1161	977	1580
1822	788	1067	1058	1290	1835	687	991	842	1222
1823	798	1066	1109	1289	1836	830	1169	1052	1637
1824	699	945	909	1033	1837	815	1155	1008	1607
1825	872	1209	1244	1830	1838	835	1211	1092	1731
1826	792	1127	1084	1333	1839	875	1290	1133	1750
1827	806	1120	997	1250	1840	703	1019	888	1543
1828	785	1070	980	1209	1841	495	753	658	982
1829	782	1077	1009	1178	1842	905	1235	1121	1791
1830	552	835	808	931	1843	836	1155	1035	1635
1831	920	1283	1288	1519	1844	871	1180	1075	1666
1832	809	1100	1009	2267	1847	815	1166	1072	1373

Blocks	*1905*	*1913*	*1921*	*1929*	*Blocks*	*1905*	*1913*	*1921*	*1929*
1848......	$ 842	$1150	$1102	$1444	1911......	$745	$941	$688	$1035
1849......	532	695	679	837	1912......	702	856	578	921
1851......	711	1130	1192	2054	1913......	648	785	538	827
1852......	647	1041	991	1416	1914......	732	869	544	937
1853......	702	1078	1035	1449	1915......	688	760	515	861
1854......	608	1013	1039	1445	1916......	702	766	519	900
1855......	670	1122	1081	1463	1917......	646	715	503	927
1856......	938	919	1157	1253	1918......	660	758	525	926
1857......	713	1112	1070	1496	1919......	509	577	469	833
1858......	572	908	894	1148	1920......	650	768	599	1040
1859......	625	901	899	1203	1921......	571	727	437	797
1860......	525	784	803	1225	1922......	701	872	745	935
1861......	557	820	812	1320	1923......	658	844	672	877
1862......	747	1064	1105	1488	1924......	782	992	761	996
1863......	734	1071	1060	1446	1925......	647	809	648	815
1864......	229	427	417	509	1926......	705	899	673	894
1867......	1025	1551	1616	2273	1927......	802	1046	779	1034
1868......	726	1204	1987	2804	1928......	804	1058	752	1049
1869......	951	1533	2146	3205	1929......	792	1103	811	1069
1870......	951	748	2099	3203	1930......	2603	3326	3480	4845
1871......	807	1288	1758	2559	1931......	1967	2534	2847	3968
1872......	973	1521	1981	3096	1932......	738	945	750	1024
1873......	988	1518	2032	3036	1933......	703	880	689	1040
1874......	985	1602	1994	3104	1934......	686	877	619	1000
1876......	926	1334	1950	3145	1935......	607	875	628	861
1877......	936	1410	1920	3221	1936......	677	844	590	933
1879......	742	1115	1391	2039	1937......	645	740	507	863
1880......	684	1140	1382	1992	1938......	649	722	524	849
1881......	831	1369	1616	2461	1939......	655	576	429	692
1882......	912	1582	1819	2767	1940......	701	790	585	1056
1883......	813	1449	1654	2354	1941......	707	826	642	1033
1884......	704	1252	1462	2050	1942......	658	777	534	879
1885......	756	1256	1350	2028	1943......	857	1084	935	1153
1887......	995	1560	1883	2295	1944......	791	1029	787	997
1888......	1229	2039	2388	2912	1945......	792	1028	722	938
1889......	1292	2013	2241	3037	1946......	757	983	692	879
1890......	1171	1777	2028	2776	1947......	751	993	730	853
1891......	1217	1799	2098	2866	1948......	626	800	633	767
1892......	1306	1938	2287	3185	1949......	680	881	753	835
1893......	1231	1978	2366	3220	1950......	502	722	620	731
1894......	1197	2006	2530	3312	1951......	833	1367	1259	2008
1895......	1295	2451	2982	3962	1952......	800	1296	1132	1911
1896......	1337	2460	2941	3953	1953......	511	746	579	788
1901......	1007	1307	1137	1630	1954......	555	886	740	918
1902......	880	1048	867	1235	1955......	470	648	497	617
1903......	551	997	794	1085	1958......	729	1024	737	947
1904......	802	1002	797	1058	1959......	546	743	569	742
1905......	728	932	811	1093	1960......	564	798	533	492
1906......	764	959	800	1036	1961......	970	1243	754	922
1907......	808	1017	800	1104	1962......	795	1408	1477	1869
1908......	691	923	667	948	1963......	718	1128	1275	1664
1909......	2600	3460	1266	4932	1964......	646	1006	949	1007
1910......	1872	2545	2407	4093	1965......	523	907	884	1283

Blocks	*1905*	*1913*	*1921*	*1929*
1966	$ 651	$1167	$1130	$1567
1967	418	711	709	849
1968	396	787	825	1056
1969	321	822	887	1103
1970	475	677	587	933
1971	143	233	220	306
1976	624	1068	1058	1363
1977	619	1079	1031	1519
1978	556	993	1019	1308
1979	614	1030	949	1323
1980	606	996	861	2279
1981	552	880	766	1238
1982	496	1024	914	1447
1986	808	866	1127	1595
1987	407	798	739	1063
1988	953	1982	1869	3015
1993	719	2070	1950	2437
1995	570	1299	1317	1806
1996	382	579	595	693
1997	354	568	544	750
1998	308	552	533	721
1999	296	556	533	774
2000	287	450	389	668
2006	556	678	410	647
2007	655	776	466	661
2008	312	444	440	486
2009	528	767	454	690
2010	540	786	470	669
2011	540	788	456	619
2012	514	798	440	605
2013	555	799	530	745
2014	494	713	485	563
2015	345	520	421	439
2023	553	830	553	750
2024	494	801	547	723
2025	494	854	581	757
2026	630	862	585	757
2027	477	704	458	681
2028	535	785	500	760
2029	447	797	528	766
2030	375	917	630	873
2031	375	857	567	842
2032	320	656	443	687
2033	268	539	366	523
2034	320	640	414	635
2035	259	541	350	530
2036	185	413	346	416
2037	222	425	310	360
2038	250	451	262	368
2041	437	716	533	756
2042	335	584	439	612
2043	370	630	499	697
2044	310	558	461	611

Blocks	*1905*	*1913*	*1921*	*1929*
2045	$ 339	$1087	$ 905	$1161
2046	518	597	521	598
2047	216	426	303	372
2051	626	1139	1164	1430
2053	684	1239	1141	1365
2054	716	1148	1064	1172
2057	186	400	397	491
2058	353	657	655	788
2059	444	764	786	934
2060	501	887	904	1066
2061	508	914	860	969
2062	494	878	816	951
2063	481	838	783	926
2064	384	653	623	737
2065	401	668	654	737
2066	288	481	465	493
2067	432	678	616	688
2068	596	975	963	1060
2069	311	494	515	579
2070	367	911	983	1147
2071	389	862	878	982
2072	306	704	716	788
2073	414	858	857	949
2074	405	880	913	1002
2075	375	1010	1047	1217
2076	494	1304	1358	1574
2077	406	1037	1221	1497
2078	451	1090	1136	1282
2079	439	1008	1005	1222
2080	458	965	928	1170
2081	456	903	892	1102
2082	443	935	893	1051
2083	344	874	762	921
2084	239	639	525	659
2109	507	987	979	1263
2110	541	853	703	920
2111	528	1088	960	886
2114	389	983	852	1068
2115	393	1087	1096	1294
2116	358	1043	1205	1382
2117	364	868	926	1055
2118	369	813	856	1044
2119	322	767	799	1002
2120	362	771	830	1113
2121	286	609	655	782
2122	588	1722	1787	2396
2123	467	1001	899	987
2125	224	540	515	591
2126	271	665	664	714
2127	266	660	683	779
2128	242	601	628	673
2129	271	645	664	720
2130	272	628	659	733

Blocks	*1905*	*1913*	*1921*	*1929*	*Blocks*	*1905*	*1913*	*1921*	*1929*
2131......	$ 217	$ 494	$ 508	$ 548	2202......	$ 47	$201	$168	$181
2141......	239	553	611	918	2203......	55	265	257	301
2143......	263	403	428	749	2213......	150	322	285	320
2144......	334	887	1111	1566	2214......	84	192	142	174
2145......	287	618	701	1044	2216......	84	203	272	276
2152......	354	768	735	812	2217......	58	291	385	529
2153......	715	1545	2287	3278	2218......	64	160	222	269
2155......	672	1164	1187	1256	2219......	62	260	301	521
2156......	194	356	370	517	2220......	96	313	392	582
2157......	629	1032	1156	1313	2221......	76	186	256	406
2158	285	490	567	681	2222......	73	241	379	536
2159......	309	670	810	1002	2223......	77	274	337	482
2160......	160	204	205	230	2224......	104	282	365	538
2162......	416	1041	2163	3154	2225......	84	223	311	408
2163......	344	851	1375	1844	2226......	71	210	396	573
2164......	170	396	551	908	2227......	62	187	284	458
2165......	243	547	981	1440	2228......	71	181	233	298
2166......	373	868	983	1264	2229......	78	228	255	302
2167......	265	453	345	536	2230......	64	179	206	269
2168......	267	572	908	1086	2231......	45	134	153	197
2181......	189	117	216	675	2232......	54	168	188	236
2185......	22	92	114	115	2233......	103	234	275	486
2186......	9	40	32	40	2234......	111	263	326	481
2187......	32	131	109	117	2235......	108	259	392	670
2196......	18	59	80	80	2236......	77	191	282	498
2197......	163	428	459	492	2238......	95	208	259	469
2198......	48	155	156	154	2239......	53	138	176	323
2199......	50	167	162	165	2240......	50	113	107	189
2200......	48	160	161	155	2241......	67	146	188	312
2201......	46	177	164	162	2242......	39	113	130	243

TABLE 5

SUMMARY. VALUES OF SELECTED BLOCKS LYING WITHIN SPECIFIED DISTRICTS IN MANHATTAN *

(000 omitted)

District	1905	1913	1921	1929
Wall Street District .... Consisting of the tip of Manhattan Island South of Fulton Street	$201,654	$260,597	$305,686	$324,465
From Fulton to 14th St. .... Bounded by the New Bowery, Bowery, and Third Ave. on the East, and by Hudson St. on the West	260,738	265,190	228,656	264,615
Eastern Border .... Between the New Bowery, Bowery, Third Avenue and the East River	125,796	155,091	126,571	142,496
Western Border .... Between Hudson St. and the Hudson River	33,836	41,141	40,881	51,531
Central Core from 14th to 25th Streets .... Between Third and Ninth Avenues	175,008	203,073	164,826	189,821
Eastern Border .... Between Third Avenue and the East River	20,129	25,528	23,460	31,345
Western Border .... Between Ninth Avenue and the Hudson River	10,362	11,909	13,414	17,060
Total Value of Central Core South of 25th St.	$637,400	$728,860	$699,168	$778,901
Total Value of Eastern Border South of 25th St.	145,925	180,619	150,031	173,841
Total Value of Western Border South of 25th St.	44,198	53,050	54,295	68,591
Total Value of Downtown Business Area	$827,523	$962,529	$903,494	$1,021,333

* Data in this table have been based upon Table 4. Total values therefore represent totals of a representative group of blocks but not of all blocks.

TABLE 5—*Continued*

District	1905	1913	1921	1929
From Twenty-fifth to Fortieth— Central Core................ Between Third and Ninth Avenues	$260,008	$430,205	$421,730	$626,949
Eastern Border .... Between Third Ave. and the East River	14,981	17,915	16,741	29,942
Western Border................ Between Ninth Avenue and the Hudson River	16,477	19,790	23,487	33,398
From Fortieth to Fifty-ninth Sts.— Central Core................ Between Third and Ninth Avenues	286,653	390,135	501,548	905,129
Eastern Border .... Between Third Avenue and the East River	21,175	24,797	24,004	74,615
Western Border................ Between Ninth Avenue and the Hudson River	24,665	32,150	40,139	62,431
Total Value of the Central Core in the Midtown District.........	$546,661	$820,340	$923,278	$1,532,078
Total Value of the Eastern Border in the Midtown District	36,156	42,712	40,745	104,557
Total Value of the Western Border in the Midtown District	41,142	51,940	63,626	95,829
Total Value of the Midtown District	$623,959	$914,992	$1,027,649	$1,732,464

TABLE 5—*Concluded*

District	1905	1913	1921	1929
Central Park Area Between 59th and 96th Streets				
Central Core .... Between Ninth Ave. and Central Park	$50,070	$62,209	$76,881	$124,039
Between Third Ave. and Central Park	195,292	214,541	229,811	392,508
Eastern Border .... Between Third Ave. and the East River	48,613	64,406	64,559	117,157
Western Border................ Between Ninth Ave. and the Hudson River	92,210	126,029	169,110	253,000
Total Value of Central Park Area.	$386,185	$467,185	$540,361	$886,704
North of 96th St. Between Lenox Ave. and the East River......	97,262	130,669	113,200	157,395
Between Lenox Ave. and the Hudson River..................	146,478	223,290	210,496	295,288
North of 155th St.	16,643	38,134	43,917	57,230
Total Value of Land North of 96th Street	$260,383	$392,093	$367,613	$509,913

TABLE 6

ASSESSED VALUATIONS OF LAND IN THE BRONX SHOWING VARIATIONS IN VALUE GROWTH IN DIFFERENT AREAS FOR SELECTED YEARS

(000 omitted)

Year	Inner Core*	Outer Circle	Periphery	Total Borough
1905.....	$79,856	$35,538	$59,606	$175,000
1913.....	131,615	82,985	117,755	332,355
1917.....	139,783	91,600	120,792	352,175
1921.....	140,626	101,108	122,881	364,615
1927.....	161,931	161,279	195,798	519,008
1929.....	176,163	198,808	283,442	658,413

* See text—page 80 for description of these terms.

TABLE 7

Assessed Valuations of Land in Brooklyn for Selected Areas

(000 omitted)

District	1905*	1910	1913	1921	1928
Borough Hall	$55,948	$61,098	$83,334	$101,194	$170,000
Broadway Area	45,636	55,675	69,413	72,440	89,662
Greenpoint, Williamsburg and Ridgewood	91,662	122,667	142,830	150,011	182,178
East New York and Cypress Hills	7,879	17,260	18,436	20,178	31,388
Flatlands		10,996	12,902	14,206	55,657
Canarsie		6,820	7,350	7,314	18,556
Bayridge, Bath Beach, Bensonhurst, Midwood, Coney Island, Sheepshead Bay	55,000	88,764	134,249	160,267	826,164

* 1905 values are estimated.

Data for Tables 6 and 7 were obtained from the city record for each specified year.

TABLE 8*

ASSESSED VALUATIONS OF LAND IN THE FIVE WARDS OF QUEENS

Wards	1906	1910	1913	1921	1926	1928
1. L. I. City	$24,091,210	$49,528,835	$63,348,645	$72,492,090	$105,311,330	$150,870,935
2. Newtown	17,427,400	40,880,205	62,212,110	77,359,095	124,731,565	167,740,030
3. Flushing	12,331,535	36,067,845	48,894,060	49,412,370	89,663,100	137,955,325
4. Jamaica	19,607,830	57,109,592	75,633,050	78,823,045	142,614,115	225,884,045
5. Rockaway	7,812,475	16,593,840	30,136,125	31,088,000	101,867,845	94,322,045
Total	$81,270,450	$200,180,317	$280,223,990	$309,174,600	$564,187,955	$776,772,380

* Data for this table were obtained from the Annual Reports of the Commissioners of Taxes and Assessments of New York City.

BIBLIOGRAPHY

Books and Monographs

Bernard, A. D., *Principles of Real Estate Valuation*, Baltimore, 1913.

Bonner, William T., *New York, The World's Metropolis 1623-1924*, New York, 1924.

Broadway Association, *Broadway, the Grand Canyon of American Business*, New York, 1926.

Dorau and Hinman, *Urban Land Economics*, New York, 1928.

Hone, Philip, *Diary of Philip Hone*, New York, 1889.

Hurd, Richard M., *Principles of City Land Values*, New York, 1905.

Lewis, Harold M., *Transit and Transportation, Regional Survey*, vol. iv, New York, 1928.

Lewis, Nelson P., *Planning of the Modern City*, p. 178, New York, 1916.

McMichael, Stanley and Bingham, Robert F., *City Growth and Values*, 1923, pp. 190-197, 231, 277.

Mitchell, Matther C., *Assessment of Property Values in American Cities*, Harvard Univ., 1929.

Regional Plan of New York and Its Environs, *Economic and Industrial Survey. The Clothing and Textile Industries*, B. M. Selekman, H. R. Walter and W. J. Couper, New York, 1927.

——, *Land Values*, H. M. Lewis, W. D. Heydecker and R. A. O'Hara, New York, 1927.

Rosewater, Victor, *Special Assessments*—a study in municipal finance, New York, 1893.

Seligman, E. R. A., *Studies in Public Finance. Reform of Municipal Taxation*, New York, 1925.

——, *Essays in Taxation*, 10th edition, New York, 1928.

Snyder, B. and Roby, R., *Fundamentals in Real Estate*, New York, 1927.

Walker, James B., *Fifty Years of Rapid Transit*, New York, 1918.

Wilgus, William J., *Proceedings of the International City and Regional Planning Conference in New York City*, April, 1925. This report also appears as a supplement to vol. iv, *Transit and Transportation, Regional Survey of New York and Its Environs*, New York, 1928.

Reports, Pamphlets and Bulletins

Annual Estimate of the Population of Queens. Queens Borough Chamber of Commerce. February, 1930.

Board of Transportation. City of New York Engineering Department. *Proposed City Subway Lines.* Drawing 526, File #49. July 29, 1927.

Brooklyn and Her Transportation Problem. Borough of Brooklyn President. Annual Report, 1906.

Building of Rapid Transit Lines in New York City by Assessment upon Property Benefited. City Club of New York. Memorandum addressed to the Board of Estimate, and the Public Service Commission. New York, Oct. 2, 1908.

Bulletin of the General Contractors' Association. New York City's New Subway System. John H. Delaney, Chairman of the Board of Transportation. New York, Dec., 1923.

Citizens' Committee on Rapid Transit. *The Rapid Transit Problem of New York.* Reports of the Committee appointed with the approval of Mayor Gaynor by the presidents of the Chamber of Commerce, and the Merchants' Association, Dec., 1910.

City Planning Procedure. Series III, #1. *Financing Improvements by Special Assessments.* Lawson Purdy, Former President of the New York City Board of Taxes and Assessments, Jan., 1926.

Control of Building Development along Rapid Transit Lines in the City of New York. Paper 206—by Edward M. Law. Proceedings of the Brooklyn Engineers' Club. New York, Jan., 1927.

Finance and Financial Administration of New York City. Recommendations and report of the sub-committee on Budget, Finance and Revenue of the City Committee on Plan and Survey. Rogers, McBain and Haig. New York, 1928.

History of Atlantic Avenue Improvement. Brooklyn Atlantic Ave. Improvement Board, 1906.

Memorandum to Mr. Fullen. Effect of Rapid Transit, projected or under construction, on assessed valuation in New York City. Board of Transportation, 1927.

Merchants' Association of New York. Committee on City Traffic. City Transit problem, pp. 5, 12, 31. New York, Jan., 1923.

Merchants Association of New York. *Subway construction number* New York, Aug., 1923.

Proceedings of the Ninth National Conference on City Planning. Kansas City, May 7-9, 1917, pp. 236-241.

Public Improvements in Manhattan. Julius Miller, President, Borough of Manhattan. New York, 1928.

Public Service Commission: First District. *Dual System of Rapid Transit for New York City.* New York, 1912.

Public Service Commission: First District. *History and Description of rapid transit routes in New York City.* New York, 1910.

Public Service Commission: First District. *History of Rapid Transit Development in the City of New York.* Louis Roth, 1917.

Rapid Transit Situation in Greater New York. Gerhard M. Dahl, Chairman of the Board of Directors of the Brooklyn-Manhattan Transit Corporation, Jan., 1927.

Report Mr. Avery M. Schermerhorn. Assessment Study #1, made by the direction of the Chairman of the Board of Transportation. New York, Aug. 31, 1925.

Report of the Committee on Rapid Transit, No. 106. American Electric Railway Association. New York, 1928.

Report of the Committee on Street Traffic Economics, No. 104. American Electric Railway Association, pp. 112-114, New York, 1928.

Report of the North Jersey Transit Commission to the Senate and General Assembly of the State of New Jersey. Jersey City, 1927.

Report of the Street Railway Commission and the Rapid Transit Commission to Honorable John C. Lodge. Mayor, Detroit, Mich., Feb., 1929.

Report to Honorable John C. Lodge, Mayor, by the Board of Street Railway Commissioners and Rapid Transit Commission on Financing a Subway Plan. Detroit, July, 1929.

Street Railways No. 7 Reform Club, New York, Feb., 1909. Municipal Affairs Committee. *A City Subway Policy*, pp. 10-16.

Transit Truths. The B. M. T. Corporation. New York, 1924.

NEWSPAPERS AND PERIODICALS

American Economic Review, vol. xviii, no. 1. Supplement March, 1928, "Papers and Proceedings of the 40th Annual Meeting of the American Economics Association," p. 5, R. M. Haig.

Brooklyn, Aug. 2, 1924, pp. 3-4, 25-30. "Should Rent Payers Pay for the Subway?", Arthur S. Somers.

Detroit Free Press, March 12, 1929, p. 12. Advertisement to Voters on the Subject of the New Subway Proposal.

Land and Freedom, July-Aug., 1925, p. 102. "New Subway Plan brings our Principles to Notice."

New York Evening Post, New York City, 1919. "Real Estate Values in Manhattan," 264 pp.

New York Herald Tribune, Dec. 9, 1929, p. 1. "Short Term Bonds for Billion Works Planned by Walker."

New York Times—

Aug. 4, 1928, p. 6xx—"Manhattan Land Values Rise with Skyscrapers. ..

Nov. 18, 1928, sec. 12, p. 1—"Farms Disappear in Dyckman area."

Mar. 24, 1929, p. 8xx—"Eighth Ave. Subway makes New Main Street."

July 28, 1929, p. 1, R. E.—"New Subways Aid in Developing Suburban Areas."

Sept. 22, 1929, p. 4xx—"Our Great Subway Network Spreads Wider."

Oct. 27, 1929, p. 4xx—"Twenty-five Years of the New York Subway."

Quarterly Journal of Economics, Aug., 1922. "Land Values in New York City," G. B. L. Arner.

Queensborough, June, 1925, pp. 384-385. "Board of Transportation Files Plans for New Rapid Transit Routes in Queensborough." Chamber of Commerce Borough of Queens.

Real Estate Magazine of New York, March, 1925, pp. 250-251, 263. "Side Light on Subways in the Present Transit Impasse," Cyrus C. Miller.

Real Estate Record and Guide—

Mar. 23, 1918, p. 6. "Transit Lines *vs.* Real Estate Values," J. Clarence Davies.

Aug. 3, 1918, pp. 119, 121. "New Subway Lines will make New York Greater."

Mar. 22, 1919, p. 365. "New Clark St. Tunnel Links West-side to Brooklyn."

Nov. 7, 1925, pp. 9-12.—"General O'Ryan Outlines Vast Improvements for Third Avenue."

Single Tax Review, Mar.-Apr., 1921, pp. 39-40. "A Suggestion for Mayor Hylan."

Reference Works, Documents, Etc.

Appleton's Dictionary of Greater New York. New York, 1903.

Boroughs of Brooklyn and Queens, Counties of Nassau and Suffolk, 1609-1924, H. I. Hazelton, 7 vols., 1925.

New York State: Laws. Chapter 545, 1915. Amendment, authorizing the use of special assessments in the construction of rapid transit facilities.

Annual Reports of the Commissioners of Taxes and Assessments of the City of New York, 1905-1928.

New York City Land Value Maps. Annual issues, 1909-1929.

New York City Department of Taxes and Assessments:

Annual *Record Books,* 1905-1929.

Manhattan Office—Municipal Building, Manhattan, 9th Floor.
Brooklyn Office—Municipal Building, Brooklyn, 2nd Floor.
Bronx Office—Tremont Ave. and Arthur Ave., 3rd Floor.
Queens Office—Long Island City.

Hyde's *Atlas of Manhattan.*
" " *The Bronx.*
" " *Brooklyn.*

" " *Queens.*
" " *Richmond.*
Transit Line Maps. Ohman Map Company.

ADDITIONAL BIBLIOGRAPHICAL SOURCES

Municipal Reference Library Notes, vol. xiii, no. 20, May 18, 1927. " Subways in the City of New York." An annotated list of selected references, 1910-1927.

Regional Survey of New York and Its Environs, vol. iv. Transit and Transportation, p. 215. Bibliography.

INDEX

Accessibility,
responsible for property values, 13, 17, 50, 74, 75, 86, 125, 126
to land not in demand has little effect on value, 50, 103, 118, 123
Ad valorem taxation, 14
Alexander Avenue, 82
Alternative to special assessments, 135-138
Arverne, 110
Assessed valuations, 25-27, 136, 142, 145-167
caution in using, 27
Astoria, 24, 111-115
Atlantic Avenue, 22, 96, 97, 100
Avenue A, 42, 68

Banking community, 35
Banking interests in the Grand Central Zone, 59
Bath Beach, 104-106
Bay Ridge, 104, 106-108
Bayside, 110
Bedford Avenue, 97
Bellaire, 120-122
Benefits to property adjacent to transit, 14, 16, 17, 32, 33, 43, 44, 51, 65, 67, 71, 74, 75, 82, 84, 86, 92, 102
Benefits vary inversely with distance from improvement, 15
Bensonhurst, 104, 105, 107
Black Belt, 71
Bloomingdale's, 59
Board of Estimate votes against special assessment device, 15
Bond issue, 136
Bond price index, 141
Boom in real estate, 27, 31, 36, 106
Borden Avenue, 113
Borough Hall, 19, 22, 23, 94, 96, 98, 122
Boston, special assessment plan, 13
Bowery, 36, 38, 42
Bridge Street, 96
Brighton Beach, 23, 104, 105
Broadway (Brooklyn), 22, 97, 98, 100, 102, 122
(Manhattan), 20, 21, 29, 37, 47, 49, 51, 52, 60, 61, 139
(Queens), 115, 116
Bronx, 79-93
map, 80
Park, 19, 21, 22, 79, 82
River, 79, 87
transit lines, 21, 22, 79, 81, 84-87
Brooklyn, 94-108
and Rockaway Beach Railway, 102
Bridge, 99
Chamber of Commerce Building, 96
map, 95
Municipal Building, 96
transit lines, 21, 22, 94, 96, 97, 99-102, 105
Brown, Frederick, 60
Buildings of large size tend to stablize land values, 34
Bushwick Avenue, 21, 98-100

Canal Street, 45
Canarsie, 102, 103
Capitalization of tax, 137
Carl Schurz Park, 67, 68
Cemetery, 108, 118, 119
Center Street Loop, 36, 99
Central core, Bronx, 79, 81, 82, 86, 89
Manhattan, 29, 36, 38, 52, 68, 69
Centralization of values, 35 (see also, concentration centers)

Central Park, 29, 45, 46, 60, 69, 73, 77
area, 66-70
area, map, 53
West, 69
Chambers Street, 39
Chanin Building, 58
Chelsea, 48
Chicago,
Mayor Dever of, 16
Report of the Subway Advisory Commission of, 16
special assessment plan, 14
Chrysler Building 58
Church Street, 45
City Club, 19, 74
City Committee on Plan and Survey, 26
City Housing Corporation, 115
City of Unrest, 38
City subway system, attempt to finance by special assessments, 15 (see also, New subway)
Clark Street, 23, 96
College Point, 109
Colorado, special assessment plan, 13
Columbus Circle, 61, 64
Concentration centers augment land values, 35, 56-60, 64, 65, 92, 94, 97, 107, 114, 120, 123, 128, 131
Coney Island, 23, 104-106
Convent Avenue, 73, 74
Corona, 24, 112, 115
Costs, of developing raw land into residential sites, 75, 76, 129
of new subway, 138
of subways compared with growth in land values, 14, 138
Court Street, 96
Culver line, 23, 105
Cypress Hills, 24, 118-120

Danahy, James W., 64
Delancey Street, 42
Delaney, John H., 15, 17
Demand for space forces up land values, 35, 48, 49, 59-63, 65, 70, 74, 94, 103, 107, 115, 123, 126, 127
Department of Taxes and Assessments, 25, 26, 142
Detroit Free Press, 14
Detroit,
Report to the Mayor, 16
special assessment plan, 14
Dever, Mayor of Chicago, 16
Ditmars Avenue, 112, 115
Dollar, change in purchasing power of, 27, 87, 129, 130, 141
Downtown business area, 29, 30, 36-50
map, 34
Dual Contracts (1913), 21, 22, 24, 85, 86, 99, 105, 112, 117
Duffus, R. L., 17
Dutch colonists, 117
Dyckman Street, 77

Early transit systems in New York, 19
Eastern Parkway, 21, 23, 99, 100
East New York, 102, 120
East River, 19, 20, 23, 32, 35, 54, 62, 63, 68, 79, 99, 110, 112
East-Side, Manhattan, 29, 38, 41, 43, 54, 61, 67, 68, 71
Eighth Avenue, 24, 30, 45, 48, 69
Association, 64
subway, attempt to finance by special assessments, 15 (see also, New subway)
Elderts Lane, 119
Electrification of roads, 19, 22, 57, 109, 121
Elevated lines, influence land values unfavorably, 54, 55, 83, 84, 91, 92, 93, 102, 108, 132
in New York City, 19-24, 30, 37, 38, 43, 47, 48, 52, 54-56, 63, 66, 68, 69, 71, 79, 81, 84-86, 89, 96, 97, 99, 101, 105, 112, 115-118
Elmhurst, 116
Environment militates against rise in value, 71, 100, 104, 118
Established sections are often slow to change when subways are built, 87, 92, 98, 123, 131

"Far East" growth, 67
Farms, 77, 121
Far Rockaway, 110
Federal Reserve Bank index, 141
Ferry (34th Street), 54, 113, 117
Fifth Avenue (Brooklyn), 22, 106-108
(Manhattan), 47, 51, 58-60, 66, 71
Financial district, 30-35, 128, 163

Financial problems in transit construction, 13
Financing of public improvements, 137
Flatbush Avenue, 23, 96, 97, 104
Flatlands, 104
Flushing, 24, 109, 116, 117
  Avenue, 97
Follow the leader, 126
Fort Hamilton, 23, 105
Fourteenth Street, Eastern Line, 21, 23, 38, 99, 100, 103, 117
Fourth Avenue (Brooklyn), 22, 23, 96, 104
  (Manhattan), 39, 47, 49, 50, 52, 54, 56
Fox Theater, 96
French, Fred, 63, 68
Fresh Pond Road, 117
Full-faith and credit bonds, 14
Fulton Street (Brooklyn), 22, 96-98, 100, 118, 120
  (Manhattan), 30, 31, 35, 36

Garden apartment community, 116
Garment Center, 40, 52, 53
General taxes, 17, 136
Glendale, 109
Grand Avenue, 115
Grand Boulevard and Concourse, 90, 91
Grand Central, 19, 21, 24, 39, 56, 57, 59, 60, 63, 128
Grand Street, 36
Graybar Building, 58
Greenpoint, 98, 99
Greenwich Village, 39, 44, 45
Greenwood Cemetery, 108
Growth in land values in New York City, 14, 27, 28, 128, 138

Haig, Robert M., 26
Harlem, 19, 66, 73
  River, 79, 80
Hearings on valuations, 136
Hewen, Loring M., 59
History of New York City transit, 19-24
Hollis, 110, 120-122
Hotel center, 58, 64
"H" system, 21
Hudson Street, 36
Hudson Tubes, 36, 51
Hunters Point, 113, 128
Hunts Point, 89
Hurd, Richard M., 126

Increment tax, 135-138
Index of purchasing power, 129
Inner core, Bronx, 79, 81, 83, 88
Insurance rates, in relation to shifts in land use, 40
Interborough, 19, 20, 23

Jackson Avenue, 112, 113, 116
Jackson Heights, 116
Jamaica, 22-24, 109, 113, 118-122, 128
  Avenue, 118, 119, 121
  Bay, 102
Jerome Avenue, 22, 90, 91

Kingsbridge Road, 91
Kissena Boulevard, 117

Land value,
  charts, 139-141
  environmental influences on effects of transit lines, 71, 93, 100, 104, 114, 118, 126, 131, 132
  fluctuating character, 28, 46, 65, 126, 127, 133
  growth in New York City, 14, 27, 28, 128, 138
  increase not due to any one factor, 77
Land values
  affected by profit making capacity, 127, 129
  arise from a conversion of land into other uses, 75-77, 83, 89, 103, 118, 124, 128, 129
  assessed, 25-27, 136, 142, 145-167
  Bronx, 81-90, 165
  Brooklyn, 96, 98, 99, 101, 103, 104, 106, 166
  Central Park Area, 66-70, 165
  consumers' choices effect upon, 126-127
  decline, 27, 28, 36, 37, 39, 41, 43, 46, 49, 106, 112, 113, 128, 129, 139-141
  Downtown business area, (Fulton–14th St.), 36, 46, 163

Land values
  Downtown business area, (14th–25th St.), 47, 49, 163
  increase, 35, 47, 48, 51-58, 60, 61, 63, 64, 67-69, 74-77, 82, 83, 86, 88-90, 101, 104, 111, 114, 115, 118, 119, 121, 124, 125, 128, 139-141, 143
  Midtown district, 51-58, 60, 61, 63, 64, 164
  North of 96th Street, 71-74, 76, 78, 165
  Queens, 28, 111-119, 121, 167
  separated from land and improvements, 27
  Wall Street district, 31-35, 163
  World War effect on, 27, 106, 129

Laurelton, 110
Law, Edward M., 41
Lease, provides for higher rent if elevated structure is removed, 55
Lefferts Avenue, 24, 118
Lenox Avenue, 21, 71, 73, 80, 84
Lewis, Nelson P., 76, 77
Lexington Avenue (Brooklyn), 22, 97
  (Manhattan), 20, 21, 37, 43, 56-60, 66, 140
Liberty Avenue, 118
Little Neck, 110
Livonia Avenue, 101, 102
Long Island City, 24, 52, 54, 109-111, 114
Long Island Railroad, 22, 97, 99, 100, 109, 113, 116-118, 121, 122
Los Angeles, special assessment plan, 13

Macy's, 51
Madison Avenue, 58-60
Main Street, 116
Main streets, 132
Manhattan Bridge, 45
Manhattan, North of 96th Street, map, 72
Market values compared with assessed valuations, 25
Men's wear industry, 40, 41
Midtown District, 29, 46, 50-65, 128
  map, 53
Midwood, 104, 106, 107

Montague Street tunnel, 21, 23, 96
Morningside Avenue, 73
Morris Avenue, 79
Murray Hill, 55
Myrtle Avenue, 22, 24, 97, 99, 117

New Lots, 23, 101
New subway, 37, 38, 45, 46, 48, 64, 69, 72, 97, 122
  attempt to finance by special assessments, 15
  cost, 138
Newtown Creek, 112, 118
New York Central Railroad, 21, 57, 58, 66, 79, 80, 83, 90
New York City,
  assessments, 26, 142-167
  growth in land values, 14, 27, 28, 128, 138
  map showing transit lines and the five boroughs, 20
  present plan of financing its subways, 17, 18
  special assessment plans, 14
New York City Club, 14, 19, 74
New York law, changes made in, 15
New York Municipal Railway Corporation, 20, 24
New York, New Haven and Hartford Railroad, 80, 88
New York Times, 17, 64, 77
Ninth Avenue, 19, 29, 48, 56, 62, 68, 69
North Jersey Transit Commission, 16
Nostrand Avenue, 98, 104
Numbered Streets
  14th St., 21, 29, 36, 37, 40, 46, 47, 61
  23rd St., 40, 48, 49, 51, 61
  25th St., 29
  33rd St., 51, 54
  34th St., 40, 52, 54, 60, 113, 117
  42nd St., 20, 21, 29, 56, 58, 60, 61, 63
  57th St., 59, 60, 62
  59th St., 20, 21, 24, 29, 56, 58, 59, 60, 62, 63, 64, 66, 69
  72nd St., 69
  79th St., 69
  86th St., 69
  96th St., 29, 57, 66, 68, 69
  138th St., (Bronx), 87

Numbered Streets
149th St. (Bronx), 84
163rd St. (Queens), 119
168th St. (Queens), 119
169th St. (Bronx), 82, 83, 90
180th St. (Bronx), 84, 85

Outer circle, Bronx, 79, 81, 88, 90

Paramount Theater, 96
Park Avenue, 20, 21, 52, 57, 58, 60, 62, 66, 71
Pay as you go policy, 138
Pelham Bay, 22, 86, 89
Pennsylvania terminal, 51, 52, 64, 113, 121, 128
Pennsylvania tunnels, 54
Periphery, Manhattan, 29
Pitkin Avenue, 101
Population, Bronx, 81
Queens, 111, 122
Post-war rise in land values, 28, 89, 103, 118, 122, 123
Potatoes, 121
Prospect Avenue, 79, 85
Prospect Park, 100, 107
Purchasing power, change in, 27, 87, 129, 130
index, 129
Purdy, Lawson, 51, 57

Queens, 109-125
Queensboro,
Bridge, 111, 112
Chamber of Commerce, 122
Corporation, 116
Plaza, 21, 24, 112, 114
Subway, 54
Queens-Boulevard, 24, 112, 115, 116, 118
Map, 110
transit lines, 21, 23, 24, 109, 112, 115-118
Queens Village, 110, 120-122

Real estate tax, 17, 136
Regional Plan of New York and Its Environs, 41, 75
Relative changes in value, 26
Removal of elevated spur, 63
Rezone Park Avenue, application to, 58
Richmond, 109, 124, 125
Richmond Hill, 24, 110, 118-120
Ridgewood, 98, 100, 117
Riverside Drive, 66, 70, 73
Rockaway, 110
Roosevelt Avenue, 24, 112, 115-118
Rosedale, 110, 120, 122

St. Albans, 120-122
St. George Hotel, 96
St. Louis, special assessment plan, 13
San Francisco
fire and earthquake, 39, 40
special assessment plan, 13
Save New York Committee, 40
Schermerhorn, Avery M., 26
Schiff Parkway, 42
Sea Beach line, 22, 23, 105
Second Avenue (Manhattan), 19, 21, 43, 50, 52, 54, 67
(Queens), 24, 112-115
Seligman, E. R. A., 135
Seventh Avenue, 20, 21, 32, 37, 38, 40, 43, 47, 49, 52, 53, 54, 56, 60
Sewerage problem in Canarsie, 104
Sheepshead Bay, 104, 106, 107
Shifts in land use, 39-41, 45, 49-52, 54, 59, 101, 118
Silk business, 39
Sinking-fund bonds, 136
Sites, most valuable in New York, 60
Sixth Avenue, 19, 21, 37, 48, 51, 52, 55, 63
Sixth Avenue elevated, attempt to finance removal by special assessments, 15
Social gains to private property owners, 135, 136
Southern Boulevard, 22, 79, 85, 87, 88
Special assessment
device rejected by Board of Estimate, 15
plans, 13, 14
Special assessments, 133, 135, 138
New York law concerning, 15
opposed by New York taxpayers, 15
principle underlying, 13
Speculative rise in land value, 51, 52, 69
Springfield, 110, 120-122
Spuyten Duyvil, 74

Stabilization of values in large built-up areas, 34, 35
Standard Bond Price index, 141
State Equalization Board, 26
Steinway tunnel, 20, 24
Stock Exchange, 30
Subdividing costs — a factor in growth of land values, 75, 76, 128, 129, 132
Subway Advisory Commission of Chicago, 16, 133
Subway does not cause increase in value, 65
"Subway-plus" concept, 50, 108
Subways in New York City, 14, 15, 17, 19-24, 29, 30, 32, 36-38, 43, 45-49, 54, 56, 58, 60, 64, 66, 68, 69, 71, 72, 86, 87, 96, 99, 100, 112
Sunnyside, 116
Sutter Avenue, 101, 102
Sutton Place, 62, 67

Tax maps, 121
Tax on annual increment in land value, 135, 136
Technique employed in calculating special assessments, 15
Tenth Avenue, 48
Theater district, 61, 94
Third Avenue (Bronx), 79, 82-84
(Manhattan), 19, 29, 36, 37, 52, 54-56, 62, 63, 67
Thirty-fourth Street Midtown Association, 54
Times Square, 21, 56, 61, 128
Transit
Committee, New York City Club, 14
Construction in New York City, 19-24
Transit lines
aid shifts in land use, 41, 42, 130
bring increased values, 13, 14, 16, 17, 18, 51, 92, 127
Central Park Area, 66, 69
construction financed by special assessments, 13
do not always bring increased values, 135
Downtown Business area (Fulton–14th St., 36-38, 43, 45, 46
Downtown Business area (14th–25th St.), 47-49
Transit lines
hasten development, 130
influence upon real estate values not uniform, 65
may draw away population, 41, 42, 100, 120
Midtown district, 54, 56, 58, 60, 61, 64
North of 96th Street, 71-72
permit emergence of land values rather than cause them, 133
transfer values rather than increase values, 130
Wall Street District, 32, 33
Transit-plus, 50, 108
Tremont Avenue, 82, 83, 85
Tudor City, 63

Utica Avenue, 23, 100, 101
Utica Avenue subway, attempt to finance by special assessments, 15

Valuable sites in New York City, 60
Van Cortlandt Park, 19, 21
Vanderbilt, Mrs., 62
Vandeveer Park, 104
Van Wyck Boulevard, 119
Varick Street, 43
Vehicular tunnel, 44, 45

Waldorf Astoria, 58
Wall Street, 29, 35, 59, 60
Wall Street District, 30-35, 128, 163
map, 31
Washington Square, 39
Webster Avenue, 79
Westchester Avenue, 21, 22, 79, 84, 85, 87, 89
West-end line, 23, 105
Westminster Heights Park, 104
West Side, Manhattan, 29, 38, 48, 61, 69, 71
White Plains Road, 22
Whitestone, 24, 109
Wholesale markets shift, 40
Williamsburgh, 98, 99
Williamsburgh Bridge, 38, 42, 99, 102
Willis Avenue, 82, 84
Willoughby Street, 96, 97
Women's garment industry, 40, 52
Woodhaven, 110, 118-120

Woodlawn, 22, 79
Woodside, 109, 116, 121
World War, effect on land values, 27, 106, 129
York Avenue, 68

Zoning laws, 123
Zukor, Adolph, 61

VITA

Edwin H. Spengler was born in Brooklyn, New York, on April 4, 1906. After completing his regular academic training in the elementary and high schools of the public school system of New York, he attended the College of the City of New York. He received his B.S. degree from the latter institution in 1925. He has since carried on his graduate work at Columbia University, where the degree of M.A. was conferred upon him in 1928. The initial steps in the preparation of the present study were made in 1927, while he was a resident at the University. For the past five years, Mr. Spengler has been a member of the staff in the Department of Economics of the College of the City of New York. His field of special interest is in real estate. He has written a monograph on Suburban Subdividing and Development in Long Island and an article on Second Mortgage Financing.